Fighting Terror Online

Martin Charles Golumbic

Fighting Terror Online

The Convergence of Security, Technology, and the Law

16100l

 Springer

Martin Charles Golumbic
Caesarea Rothschild Institute
University of Haifa
Mount Carmel, Haifa 31905, Israel
golumbic@cs.haifa.ac.il

ISBN: 978-0-387-73577-1   e-ISBN: 978-0-387-73578-8

Library of Congress Control Number: 2007936872

Printed on acid-free paper.

9 8 7 6 5 4 3 2 1

springer.com

Foreword

This book finds its roots in the horror that engulfed us all around the globe as we experienced and watched with disbelief the events of September 11, 2001. Naturally, policy-makers around the world rushed to examine their law enforcement capabilities and the suitability of these tools to the new *war on terror*. This examination resulted in a wave of legislation around the world, aimed at increasing the power of law enforcement agencies. The digital environment was a major focus of these regulatory and legislative attempts. Given the horror of the events and the haste to provide law enforcement agencies with the best tools possible to fight the new threat, policy-makers moved forward without much public discussion. Legislators around the world rushed to do the same. No real public debate took place before the USA PATRIOT Act was approved by Congress, 6 weeks after 9/11.[1] Our concern is that the public's voice is also needed in this process.

Once the sky over Manhattan cleared a bit, it was time for us to take a step back and assess the fallout from that horrific day. As academics who focus on digital law, my colleagues Michael Birnhack and Niva Elkin-Koren, focused their attention on examining how the events and the war on terror that followed affected the digital environment, especially the Internet, and what would be their future effects. We decided to explore these issues in a unique academic forum, together with students of the Faculty of Law and co-sponsored by the Caesarea Edmond de Rothschild Foundation Institute for Interdisciplinary Applications of Computer Science at the University of Haifa, Israel. A group of 17 outstanding students, some of whom were jointly majoring in law and computer science,

---

[1] Uniting and Strengthening America by Providing Appropriate Tools Required to Intercept and Obstruct Terrorism Act, 2001, Pub. L. No. 107-56, § § 105, 201–202, 204, 212, 814, 115 Stat. 272 (2001).

participated in a research seminar during the fall semester of 2001. The goal was defined as the formulation of an appropriate policy at the interface between security and technology, human rights and economic policy. Research was conducted in teams, followed by group discussions. To complete the research stage and to learn about the views of experts and professionals working in these areas, we organized a workshop (Shefayim, December 26–27, 2001) where dozens of researchers and practitioners from various areas of computer science, law, communications and media, strategic studies and philosophy met for two intense days of discussions. Lawyers and jurists came from academia, from the private sector, and from the public sector – with representatives from the Israeli Ministries of Justice, Defense, and Communication – to discuss their experiences and views. We also heard the opinions of those who are directly involved in the digital environment, including researchers in the field of encryption, defense personnel, lawyers, and businesspeople. An exceptional dynamic was created over the two days of informative lectures and fruitful discussions, making absolutely clear the need for independent discussion and interdisciplinary research on issues related to law and technology.

Following the research workshop and the forum, a Hebrew-language position paper was authored and distributed to policy-makers and others in Israel. Continuing in this direction, Elkin-Koren and Birnhack conducted further research, which resulted in an article on the *Invisible Handshake*,[2] addressing vital issues on the role of knowledge in the global world and the reemergence of the State in the digital environment.

Pursuing such interdisciplinary aspects of law, technology and computer science, this book evolved and developed into a volume whose topics are of concern and interest to a worldwide audience. The book provides a snapshot of the legal regime in the 9/11 aftermath and a general framework for understanding the emerging legal and technological issues. The legal response to online security threats is gradually maturing and will evolve further in the coming decade. The fundamental principles, however, are likely to remain the same.

---

[2] Michael D. Birnhack & Niva Elkin-Koren, *The Invisible Handshake: The Reemergence of the State in the Digital Environment,* 8 Virginia J. of Law and Tech. no. (6), (2003), 1–57.

Preface

The unprecedented events that have taken place in recent years have led legislators and governments throughout the world to reconsider and restructure their policies regarding security issues. Today, worldwide attention is being given to a new security threat, in the form of global terrorism. Legal systems are being called upon to provide a response to these threats, in all areas of life, including the online environment.

Among its many tools, global terror also uses advanced technological methods. This fact presents a difficult challenge to policymakers. Therefore, we have chosen to focus this book on the issue of formulating appropriate policy at the interface between security and technology, human rights and economic policy.

The fundamental issue – the tension between security needs and civil rights – is not new. A great deal of experience has been amassed in various countries in this regard, and the question that now arises is whether the existing system of principles and laws, developed on the basis of experience gathered in the "concrete" world, is applicable to the "digital" environment.

This book presents the position that the online environment is a significant and relevant theater of activity in the fight against terror, and will identify the threats, the security needs, and the issues that are unique to this environment. We examine whether the unique characteristics of this environment require new legal solutions, or whether existing solutions are sufficient. Three areas of online activity are identified that require reexamination: security, monitoring, and propaganda. For each of these, we will indicate the issues, examine existing legal arrangements, and offer guidelines for formulating legal policy. There is a demonstrated need to relate to the digital environment as a battlefront, map the new security threats, and thereby hope to provide focus to the pressing discussion on today's legislative and technological agenda.

Acknowledgments

We are proud to acknowledge the University of Haifa students who, under the guidance of Dr. Michael Birnhack and Prof. Niva Elkin-Koren, co-authored the original Hebrew position paper aimed at policy-makers, and whose work inspired and served as the basis for this research: Eran Aloni, Rachel Aridor, Eran Bar-Or, Yael Bregman, Udi Einhorn, Keren Elisha, Gal Eschet, Alon Fiul, Haviva German, Eyal Greener, Shahar Grinberg, Efy Michaeli, Tal Ron, Nir Segal, Miri Shai, Asaf Zabari, and Ben Zohar.

The Workshop and Forum, which served as the incubators for this book, took place thanks to the generous support of the Caesarea Edmond Benjamin de Rothschild Foundation Institute for Interdisciplinary Applications of Computer Science at the University of Haifa. We would like to express our appreciation to the Institute and its sponsors.

A distinguished list of experts contributed time and energy to the Forum and Workshop making valuable contributions. The participants gave definition to the questions under discussion, presented a range of viewpoints regarding the issues on the agenda, and offered a clearer perspective on points that were still ambiguous. We would like to thank all of them (in alphabetical order): Professor Niv Ahituv, Mr. Oded Cohen, Professor Amos Fiat, Dr. Irith Hartman, Dr. Daphne Lamish, Dr. Fania Oz-Salzberger, and Professor Gabi Weimann.

Translating and editing the original position paper required a great deal of work, and we would like to thank Miriam Daya, Stephanie Nakache, and Perry Zamek. For the task of expanding, researching and rewriting the position paper into book form, we would especially like to acknowledge and thank our research assistants Sara Kaufman and Yael Bregman-Eschet, as well as Diane Romm for the final editing.

The framework of the current book benefited from the evolving research on the topic by my distinguished colleagues Michael Dan Birnhack and Niva Elkin-Koren. It would have been impossible to bring this book to light without their leadership in this area. As the co-directors of the Center for Law and Technology at the University of Haifa, they are inspiring a new generation of researchers with new challenges, ideas and questions to be solved. They would especially like to thank Yochai Benkler, Robert Brauneis, Julie Cohen, Amitai Etzioni, Michael Froomkin, Ellen Goodman, Irit Haviv-Segal, Orin Kerr, Neil Netanel, Dawn Nunziato, David Post, Joel Reidenberg and the participants at the *Public Design Workshop* at NYU School of Law, Rutgers Law School Faculty Colloquium, the Dean Dinwoodey Center for Intellectual Property Studies at George Washington University Law School, the *Telecommunication Policy Research Conference* (September 2002), the joint colloquia of the Faculties of Law at the University of Haifa and Tel Aviv University, and the Privacy Symposium: *Securing Privacy in the Internet Age* (Stanford Law School, March 2004).

Contents

Introduction

In recent years, it has become tragically apparent that terrorism is a global phenomenon. The response – the *war on terror* – has thus, unsurprisingly and necessarily, become global too.[1] When terrorism takes place in public spaces, shopping malls, subways, buses, restaurants and cafes, the *war on terror* takes the form of camera monitors, airport checks, data surveillance, and the increased presence of security forces in all these spaces. Terrorists make use of the public media by relying on the certainty that their brutal acts will be reported in headline news, so they can capture the front page to achieve their political gains. The *war on terror* then responds with hot debates in newspaper columns, television talk shows, radio call-in shows, documentary movies, and public squares. Whether it is London's Hyde Park or a regular park bench of the elderly in Smallville, all of these attributes reflect the characteristics of modern wars, or perhaps post-modern warfare. They are no longer limited to a geographic "front;" the enemy is not always a visible army, and in some cases, it is not always possible to identify the enemy at all.

Global Wars in a Global Information Environment

The global *war on terror* is a war orchestrated by national states that are increasingly losing their role as the centers of power in modern times. Redefining national borders is no longer the goal of the new global war.

---

[1] The term "war on terror" is controversial in itself, and "terrorism," too, is difficult to define. The term "war on terror" has been applied in many contexts over the past century. This book uses the term as it was first applied by President George W. Bush in his address to a joint session of Congress on September 20, 2001. See http://www.whitehouse.gov/news/releases/2001/09/20010920-8.html.

M. C. Golumbic, *Fighting Terror Online.*
© Springer 2008

Terrorists often set a far more ambitious objective for themselves, that of shaking the fundamental principles of the free world and setting new cultural hegemonies. Terrorism threatens civilians, everywhere and nowhere in particular. Individuals still seek security across national borders. States, however, can no longer provide a remedy against terror and, unfortunately, too often fail to secure the personal safety of their citizens. The enemy becomes an undefined "them," while we remain "we." Old dichotomies and long-established, bloody "principles of war" collapse, while new ones emerge to replace them.

The new *war on terror* takes place in yet another arena, the digital information environment, namely the Internet. The use of means of communications in the context of war is not new. Wherever communications have been used in the battlefield, they have also been a target. This is true of the pigeon carrying a message between the king and his soldiers, of human messengers running between camps, of the telegraph, the telephone, the radio, and recently the Internet. A message can kill; a message can save lives. It is a target and a crucial tool, always an enigma to be deciphered, interpreted and applied.

War and technology have always walked hand in hand. The machinery of war is considered one of the most powerful, motivating forces of technological progress. Most technologies have been developed as tools for warfare, been adopted as such soon after being developed in the non-military market, or been created as a spin-off of warfare research.[2] The Internet is no different. This seemingly civilian and egalitarian information environment was conceived and born as a defensive infrastructure, to be resilient to attacks by the enemy.[3] It is now also being used by the new enemy, and law enforcement has no choice but to follow the terrorists, treating the Internet as a war zone.

Yet, the extension of the current *war on terror* into the Internet is not just another development in the linear history of technological progress and war. Fighting terrorism today is unlike any other war in history. Much of the difference lies in the unique characteristics of the digital environment, which has tremendous potential and power to change the way in which we live. Within the very first few minutes of their first Internet use, most users realize its special nature and its potential for humankind. It

---

[2] For the history of war and technology and their complex relationship, see Martin L. van Crevald, Technology and War: From 2000 B.C. to the Present (New York, 1991).

[3] See Richard T. Griffiths, *History of the Internet, Internet for Historians, Chapter Two: From ARPANET to World Wide Web* (2002), available at http://www.let.leidenuniv.nl/history/ivh/chap2.htm.

is already apparent that the digital environment is reshaping our personal lives, our political institutions and organizational structures, our habits and economy. Now it is also a war zone.

Cyberspace is filled with a myriad of targets for terrorists and creates a new type of vulnerability in modern societies. As Thomas Ridge, former Director of Homeland Security, who emphasized America's critical need for a coordinated, comprehensive national strategy to protect against terrorist threats and attacks, noted:

> Information technology pervades all aspects of our daily lives, of our national lives. Its presence is felt almost every moment of every day, by every American. It pervades everything from a shipment of goods, to communications, to emergency services, and the delivery of water and electricity to our homes. All of these aspects of our life depend on a complex network of critical infrastructure information systems. Protecting this infrastructure is critically important.
>
> Disrupt it, destroy it or shut down these information networks, and you shut down America as we know it and as we live it and as we experience it every day. We need to prevent disruptions; and when they occur, we need to make sure they are infrequent, short and manageable. This is an enormously difficult challenge. It is a technical challenge, because we must always remain one step ahead of the hackers.
>
> It's a legal challenge, because this effort raises cutting-edge questions of both privacy and civil liberties. It's a political challenge, because the government must act in partnership with the private sector, since most of the assets that are involved in this effort are owned by the private sector, which owns and operates the vast majority of America's critical infrastructure.[4]

This book explores the intersection where the *war on terror* meets the digital environment. Once we replace our enthusiasm for the tremendous educational, political, cultural, and social opportunities in the digital environment with the new mindset of the law enforcement agents who are responsible for the safety of the citizenry, the Internet no longer seems a garden of roses. The digital environment, like other civil spheres, hosts a mixture of obedient citizens and covert terrorists, mingled therein, who utilize the Net for their vicious purposes. It has a dual nature, as it simultaneously hosts users with benevolent intentions and those who use it to wreak destruction. Therefore, the innocent public arena necessarily becomes the object of law enforcement efforts. Once it was the pigeon, the messenger delivering secrets among the battle stations, that was targeted by enemy intelligence. If it were caught, the harm was the disclosure of the information carried by the bird. However, Internet communication is

---

[4] See White House, Office of the Press Secretary, News Release, Oct. 9, 2001, available at http://www.whitehouse.gov/news/releases/2001/10/20011009-4.html.

not a pigeon. It is the engine of civilization in post-modern times. If it is shot down or intercepted, it is not just the carrier that loses; we all lose. Of course, we cannot afford to shut down the Internet, so the question becomes how the bird can be captured without killing it. Herein lies the dilemma to be explored in the chapters that follow.

The Decline of the State

The *war on terror* sheds light on and challenges the role of the State – any state – in the digital environment. By "State" we mean the democratic system of government, which is elected by the people to govern themselves, a government that, in liberal democracies, acts as the representative of the people itself. The development of the digital environment during the last decade of the twentieth century is associated with a general decline in the role of the State.

By the end of the twentieth century, it seemed that we had entered a post-national era. The advances of technology mean that citizens rely less on the State to provide various needs. Once communications, commerce, education and consumption of information, culture and entertainment are conducted over international networks, *physical borders matter less and less*.[5] Some governments around the world realized this immediately and sought to limit their citizens' access to the Internet. A Chinese surfer has a very different Internet experience than that of a French surfer, not to mention an Iranian or a North Korean versus an Italian.[6] Some states have attempted to reinstate or transpose the physical borders into cyberspace. The well-known decision of French courts to require U.S.-based Yahoo! to prevent French surfers from accessing Nazi memorabilia on Yahoo!'s auction site is a clear illustration,[7] as is Google's reported agreement to

---

[5] See David R. Johnson & David G. Post, *Law and Borders: The Rise of Law in Cyberspace*, 48 Stan. L.Rev. 1367 (1996); BORDERS IN CYBERSPACE: INFORMATION POLICY AND THE GLOBAL INFORMATION INFRASTRUCTURE (Brian Kahin & Charles Nesson, eds., MIT Press, 1997).

[6] See the country studies performed by the OpenNet Initative, available at http://www.opennetinitiative.net.

[7] See the decision in France: League Against Racism and Anti-Semitism (LICRA) v. Yahoo! Inc., Yahoo! France (County Court, Paris, 20.11.00), available at http://www.lapres.net/yahen11.html, and a related decision on the enforceability of the French decision in the United States: Yahoo! Inc. v. La Ligue Contre Le Racisme Et L'Antisemitisme, 433 F.3d 1199 (9th Cir. 2006), *cert. denied*, La Ligue Contre le Racisme et l'Antisemitisme v. Yahoo! Inc., 126 S.Ct. 2332 (2006). For a discussion, see Joel R. Reidenberg, *Yahoo and Democracy on the Internet*, 42 JURIMETRICS 261 (2002).

censor the search results of Chinese users.[8] *The New York Times* limited the access of British users to a story about a pending terror investigation in the UK, citing adherence to local UK sub-judice law.[9] These cases illustrate the tension between global technology and the local sovereignty of states. States lose their power when faced with borderless alternatives, and almost instinctively, attempt to hold on to their territorial power and re-establish it in the online environment.

The State's loss of power also raises some doubts as to the very legitimacy of the State. If it no longer plays a fundamental role in our lives, perhaps the State is obsolete. While this is obviously an extreme claim, one to which we do not subscribe, it might imply that in particular areas, the State, which functions through the rule of law within national borders, may no longer be useful in Cyberland. Consider the contours of free speech, for instance. A state may attempt to regulate obscenity and declare all obscene content not to be "speech" for the purpose of its free speech jurisprudence. This is the legal situation in the United States. Such a declaration results in a legal debate as to the definition of obscenity, but that is an American debate.[10] The point here is that once access to obscene material is easily available through the Internet, the local definitions – whatever they are – no longer matter. Or, consider another example–virtual casinos. Once citizens realize that they can gamble online, while physically located in their "no-gambling allowed" state, it suddenly seems that the old rule is no longer valid. Of course, we might re-validate it, for example by imposing duties on financial intermediaries,[11] but the doubts raised by the new technologies are arrows shot at the core of the legitimacy of the State.

States have also lost power to corporations. As local corporations grow into giant global, multinational entities, operating in many countries, they can juggle funds and activities between them. Some of the biggest global corporations have become so powerful that they are richer than most states, and they have learned that they can manipulate local governments

---

[8] *See* Michael Liedtke, *Google Agrees to Censor Results in China, AP*, Jan. 24, 2006, available at http://msl1.mit.edu/furdlog/docs/2006-01-25_apwire_google_cn.pdf

[9] *See* Tom Zeller, *Times Withholds Web Article in Britain*, New York Times, August 29, 2006.

[10] The current judicial test to determine the contours of obscenity were outlined in Miller v. California, 413 U.S. 15 (1973). The Supreme Court struggled with its application to cyberspace. In the context discussed here, an interesting controversy revolved around one element of the *Miller* test, that which addresses "contemporary community standards." How should a "community" be identified on the Internet? *See* Ashcroft v. American Civil Liberties Union, 535 U.S. 564 (2002).

[11] See Unlawful Internet Gambling Enforcement Act of 2006, codified as 31 U.S.C. §§ 5361–5367.

to meet their needs. When some developed countries pushed for a new global order in intellectual property laws, for example, they were impelled to do so by the multinational corporations acting from within these countries.[12] The rise of multinational corporations is the result of many factors, with the information-based economy and global technologies comprising just two aspects thereof. Whatever the reasons may be, however, the result is that the State has lost power.

Yet another reason for the demise of the power of the State is that new technologies offer *code* as a substitute for the main tool of governance that the State traditionally held – the law. Joel Reidenberg pointed to *Lex Informatica*, [13] and Lawrence Lessig coined the phrase "*code is law.*"[14] Technology, goes the argument, affects the way in which we behave no less than state-issued laws. In many cases, code actually replaces the law. Where the law fails to protect our privacy, Privacy Enhancing Technologies (PETs) attempt to provide an answer. When copyright owners are disappointed with the legal protection provided by the State, they turn to Digital Rights Managements (DRMs) to fill in the void. The result is the commodification of information, at the expense of a free, open commons.[15] Contracts embedded in code are self-executed, meaning that the parties no longer rely on the State to provide enforcement. Instead, it is code that serves as the solution. The overall consequence is that the Internet, a distributed network that belongs to no one and is run by no government, is packed with the commercial interests of multinational corporations who have only one goal: promoting their own self-interests. This is where the decline of the State is most visible.

The Comeback of the State

Faced with the decline of their power, states have found themselves weaker than ever before and unequipped to face the new global terrorism. The decline of the State in the digital environment reached its lowest point

---

[12] See Pamela Samuelson, *The Copyright Grab*, Wired 4.01 (1996); Peter Drahos, *Negotiating Intellectual Property Rights: Between Coercion and Dialogue, in* Global Intellectual Property Rights: Knowledge, Access and Development 161 (Peter Drahos & Ruth Mayne, eds., 2002).

[13] Joel R. Reidenberg, *Lex Informatica: The Formulation of Information Policy Rules through Technology, 76 Texas* L. Rev. 553 (1998).

[14] Lawrence Lessig, CODE AND OTHER LAWS OF CYBERSPACE (New York, Basic Books, 1999).

[15] For a critical analysis of the process of commodification, see The Commodification of Information (Niva Elkin-Koren & Neil Netanel, eds., Kluwer Information Law Series, 2002). For a discussion of the counter-forces pushing towards a commons-based environment, see Yochai Benkler, THE WEALTH OF NETWORKS (2006).

just before the realization that a new kind of threat was at work – that of global terrorism. Moreover, a new type of war – a *war on terror* – would be required in response to the threat, despite the lack of agreement on how such a war should be handled.

Faced with new threats of global terrorism and the need to undertake enforcement measures in the online environment, governments around the world found themselves struggling to reinstate their power in the digital environment. Some would argue that this process was, and still is, inevitable, and that the *war on terror* merely serves as a cover for the continued attempts by states to assert their control over a network that remains out of reach for local governments and threatens their sovereignty.

However, traditional governmental tools do not fit the new digital arena. During the temporary absence of the State from the information arena, the latter has changed. Perhaps it has not yet fully matured, but the information arena has surely developed some habits. There are powerful private entities in this arena, and many of these have acquired their power by pushing governments to change their internal laws in favor of these influential groups. Intellectual property laws, especially copyright laws, and rules regulating the liability of Online Service Providers (OSPs) are chief examples[16], as well as new rules governing online commercial competition, such as the new life of the ancient tort of *trespass to chattels*.[17]

Governments wishing to regain control must adapt to the new situation. The State has done so by holding hands with the private nodes of power. The *invisible handshake*[18] between the market and the State represents the cooperation between governments and large market players that emerged in the information environment during the late 1990s. While this partnership is significant, it is invisible to most users. As Richard Clarke, former special advisor to President Bush for Cyber Security, appointed shortly after 9/11, warned:

"America has built cyberspace, and America must now defend its cyberspace. But it can only do that in partnership with industry. [...] Private sector companies own and operate most of our critical infrastructure

---

[16] Niva Elkin-Koren, *Copyright Law and Social Dialogue on the Information Superhighway: The Case Against Copyright Liability of Bulletin Board Operators*, 13 Cardozo Arts & Ent. L.J. 345 (1995).

[17] Niva Elkin-Koren, *Let the Crawlers Crawl: On Virtual Gatekeepers and the Right to Exclude Indexing*, 26 U. Dayton L. Rev. 179 (2001).

[18] Michael D. Birnhack & Niva Elkin-Koren, *The Invisible Handshake: The Reemergence of the State in the Digital Environment*, 8 Virginia J. of Law and Tech. no. 6 (2003), 1–57.

cyberspace systems. So we have been working closely with industry. [. . .] We'll be working even more with them in the future, to secure our cyberspace from a range of possible threats, from hackers to criminals to terrorist groups, to foreign nations, which might use cyber war against us in the future."[19]

The *invisible handshake* is a simple phenomenon, yet a disturbing one, because it makes the State reliant on the cooperation of corporations for executing some of its basic roles, such as regulation and enforcement. Such is the case when online service providers are asked to report suspicious behavior to the authorities or are asked to implement various filtering systems. Privatizing the State's enforcement functions liberates law enforcement agencies from some of the restraints that limit the exercise of power by governments. It therefore renders useless some traditional checks and balances that safeguard individual liberty and provide guarantees against governmental abuse of power. When dot.com holds hands with dot.gov, law enforcement tasks are de-facto privatized to non-elected, commercially motivated entities, accountable to no one. The State is back in the picture, but in a completely new way. One of the main tools that the State has traditionally used to perform its designated tasks is the law. The American founding fathers taught us that the government is one of laws, not of men. The powers of the State were determined by the law, examined under the law, and limited by the law. The law served as a space where old war-related dilemmas were addressed. The law is also the language of the *invisible handshake* and occupies the space where the current comeback of the State is taking place. When the state acts indirectly through private corporations, it bypasses the fundamental checks and balances set in constitutional law.

Balancing Wars through the Law

Wartime dilemmas are not a new phenomenon. How should a sovereign country treat civilian populations in an occupied territory during wartime? How should prisoners of war be treated, particularly if they are believed to have information that can save many lives (the "ticking bomb" case)? As

---

[19] *See* White House, Office of the Press Secretary, News Release, Oct. 9, 2001, available at http://www.whitehouse.gov/news/releases/2001/10/20011009-4.html.

the war extends beyond the battlefield itself, what are the ethical, political, or legal limits?[20]

Propaganda and other means of psychological warfare raise yet another set of problems. Can a government deliberately circulate disinformation in order to mislead the enemy, even though it may confuse or mislead its own people? Can the press report everything that it knows? Is information about military activity fit to print? Is there a limit to the freedom of speech of citizens who object to the war and openly support the enemy or who may even urge soldiers to disobey their commanders? These and many other issues cannot be ignored. Many of the answers are difficult to find. Usually, the places to which we look in our search for answers are in ethics, politics, and perhaps justice.

The law is often the focal point where all these considerations converge. A constitution often reflects the morality of the people, and courts strive to interpret it to maintain its integrity to this morality.[21] Where politicians often limit their view to the "here and now" – with their horizons often not extending beyond the next elections – the law has the ability to consider both the immediate problem and the long-term implications thereof. This is by no means an easy task. Courts often lack the ability and expertise to evaluate military needs. They are often hesitant, as they should be, and are frequently afraid to make bold decisions when it comes to military issues. This is only natural and understandable. Few are willing to take the risk when human lives are at stake. It is thus not surprising that courts seek "escape routes," usually in doctrines of non-justiciability.

However, sometimes courts do not have the luxury of avoiding the hard cases. They might turn to international law, but often it is constitutional law that serves as the legal framework for addressing war-related dilemmas. During World War II, the U.S. Supreme Court approved the detention of American citizens of Japanese origin, in the notorious *Korematsu* case.[22] While the case is considered one of the darkest decisions of the U.S. Supreme Court, it is also regarded as a paradigm of an elaborate methodology of constitutional balancing. Today, this method is utilized in many legal systems in liberal democracies. For example, the European Convention on Human Rights (ECHR) reflects the understanding that human rights are not absolutes and that on some occasions rights need to

---

[20] *See* Gabriel Weimann, TERROR ON THE INTERNET: THE NEW ARENA, THE NEW CHALLENGES (USIP Press Books, 2006).

[21] For constitutional interpretation based on morality, see Ronald Dworkin, FREEDOM'S LAW: THE MORAL READING OF THE AMERICAN CONSTITUTION (Harvard University Press, 1996).

[22] *See* Korematsu v. United States, 323 U.S. 214 (1944).

be balanced against each other. Sometimes it is a social need that requires compromising on human rights. Freedom of the press can be halted in order to avoid disclosing a secret military operation as it is taking place. The privacy of suspects may be violated if there is a reasonable basis for believing that they are hiding crucial enemy secrets. Sometimes liberty itself may be compromised in order to extract vital information from a suspect, such as knowledge of a bomb about to explode on a city bus (the "ticking bomb problem").

These constitutional tools provide a framework for the law in regulating some-war-related dilemmas. Surely, not all problems can be solved in solemn judicial chambers. In many cases, the balancing of military interests with human rights is so difficult that it is almost unbearable. However, we may be comforted by the fact that legal systems have gained knowledge and experience in dealing with these complex matters. As legal systems have learned from each other's experience, especially since the end of World War II, our legal understanding of human rights continues to develop and the law is better equipped to address these questions.

Digital Law

Today, liberal democracies are faced with a new kind of war – the *war on terror* – and a new battlefield – the Internet. Are the old laws of war still relevant? In answering this question, we need to bear in mind the complex and dialectic relationship between law and technology. It is wrong as a matter of description and useless as a matter of normative judgment to declare that one of the two rivals – law or technology – trumps the other.[23]

Indeed, it is often the case that the law is challenged by new technologies. In this sense, the law often lags behind new technologies. Most legal rules were drafted before the advent of the Internet. For instance, how does copyright law apply in the digital environment? Simple acts that do not trigger copyright issues at all in the physical world, such as lending a book to a friend, might suddenly be treated as copying, publishing, distributing, or displaying to the public when performed in the digital context. In response to the new environment, some rules have been drafted to address problems such as those related to defamatory speech posted on a website. Should the law treat the website operator as it treats the publisher

---

[23] Niva Elkin-Koren, *Making Technology Visible: Liability of Intent Service Providers for Peer-to-Peer Traffic*, 9 NYU J. OF LEGIS. AND PUBLIC POLICY 15 (2006).

of a book or a newspaper? Should ISPs be exempted from liability for any injurious materials exchanged by their patrons?[24] The law, by its very nature, is often called upon to address disputes over uses of new platforms and therefore must respond to the challenges of new technologies.

Sometimes new rules are drafted by the legislature, and other times courts interpret old rules so that they fit the new technology. Some of these new or renewed rules might fail, but then they will be replaced by even newer ones. The American experience with regulating children's access to online pornography is an example.[25] In yet other cases, technology responds to the legal rule. The rise of non-centralized peer-to-peer file-sharing systems, like Kazaa after the legal defeat of Napster, is a well-known example.[26] Finally, in some cases, technology may substitute for law. Code may replace law in protecting privacy, as in the cases of Privacy Enhancing Technologies (PETs) such as P3P and anonymizer.com.[27] Rather than imposing access restrictions to online materials, one may simply use a filter. Instead of prohibiting unauthorized copying, Digital Rights Management systems, used in formats such as eBooks and pdf files, may limit the technical ability to redistribute or make copies. In this sense, code becomes law. However, even this type of regulation by code would be subject to the law and its underlying principles.

---

[24] See 47 U.S.C. § 230, and its interpretation in Zeran v. America Online, Inc., 129 F.3d 327 (4th Cir. 1997). See also Batzel v. Smith, 333 F.3d 1081 (9th Cir. 2003), and compare it to the European solution to the problem of ISP liability, in Directive 2000/31/EC of the European Parliament and of the Council of 8 June 2000 on Certain Legal Aspects of Information Society Services, in particular Electronic Commerce, in the Internal Market (Directive on Electronic Commerce), articles 12–15.

[25] Congress and the Courts are still engaged in a 10-year old struggle in which Congress enacts laws that are then invalidated by the courts. This process is repeated over and over, generally with Congress losing the battle. For example, Congress enacted the Communications Decency Act of 1996 (CDA), which was declared unconstitutional in Reno v. ACLU, 929 F. Supp. 824 (E.D. Pa., 1996), aff'd, Reno v. ACLU, 521 U.S. 844 (1997). Following these decisions, Congress enacted the Child Online Protection Act (COPA), which, after several tests in the lower courts and the Supreme Court, is still under preliminary injunction. See American Civil Liberties Union v. Reno, 31 F.Supp.2d 473 (E.D.Pa. 1999), aff'd, American Civil Liberties Union v. Reno, 217 F.3d 162 (3rd Cir., 2000), reve'd, Ashcroft v. American Civil Liberties Union, 535 U.S. 564 (2002); remanded, American Civil Liberties Union v. Ashcroft, 322 F.3d 240 (3rd Cir. 2003), aff'd and remanded, Ashcroft v. American Civil Liberties Union, 542 U.S. 656 (2004). At the time of this writing, the trial on the merits of the case is taking place in the District Court (Oct. 2006).

[26] See A&M Records, Inc. v. Napster, Inc., 239 F.3d 1004 (9th Cir. 2001). Later cases discussed various other p2p systems, finding they violate copyright. In re Aimster Copyright Litigation, 334 F.3d 643 (7th Cir. 2003); Metro-Goldwyn-Mayer Studios, Inc. v. Grokster Ltd 125 S.Ct. 2764 (2005).

[27] See http://www.anonymizer.com/ and http://www.w3.org/P3P/ respectively.

When new laws are made, be it by the legislature, courts, or the executive branch, and when we evaluate new laws, we need to bear this complex relationship in mind. Laws reflect ideology, ethics, social norms, and cultural values. They have a goal and a purpose, namely, to improve our lives in the community. The law is a fundamental social instrument in modern democracies, a fact that is sometimes forgotten. Hence, we should not seek to get rid of our laws too quickly. We should decipher them and study their underlying purpose. We should then study the new technologies, the opportunities that are embedded within them and the values that they reflect, as well as their negative consequences. When devising legal solutions, one should bear in mind that whatever stance is chosen, it is likely to have an effect. Technology might respond to a law in a way that would render the law obsolete within 10 minutes after it takes effect. We should seek solutions by going back and forth between the law, with its social goals, and technology, including its opportunities and negative consequences, in order to find the equilibrium between them.

The Law of Digital Wars

This book attempts to tie together three elements that converge here: security, technology, and the law. Should the law regulate the conflicts between national security needs and human rights when it comes to the digital environment? How can it best do so? What is the golden path that will allow us to achieve our optimal security goals while causing minimal harm to our civil activities, which all take place in the same arena? These issues are put in the context of the new threats posed by global terrorism and the *war on terror*, as well as the decline of the State and its reemergence in the digital environment. It is the context of a dynamic technology that interacts dialectically with the law.

An Outline of the Book

We begin by outlining the framework of this book, that is, the comeback of the State in the digital environment. Chapter 1 will present the main theme of the book – the balance between the need for security and the safeguarding of civil liberties. We will first map the threats, both physical and virtual, particularly in the areas of data protection and monitoring of information, and then address the issues of psychological and informational warfare, with a focus on propaganda. Security threats within the online environment can also be classified based on the type of damage caused, whether physical or non-physical. In the category of non-physical damage, we can include the term *soft war*, referring to the dissemination of false information for propaganda purposes and demoralization. The legal problems that arise in connection with the issues of incitement, sedition, disinformation, hostile propaganda, and hate speech have been dealt with in depth in the pre-digital environment. Within that framework, many legal systems have devised a series of constitutional balances to guide both the executive and the judiciary branches. The issues covered include the tension between security needs and the freedom of the press, the public interest in the maintenance of order versus the freedom to demonstrate, and the limits on forms of political expression that offend the majority. The chapter continues with a discussion of the preservation of civil liberties in the information age. Individual subsections will deal with topics about the right to privacy, freedom of speech, freedom of occupation, market intervention and research and development considerations, and the influence of encryption regulation on electronic commerce.

Building on this theoretical basis, Chapter 2 demonstrates how legal systems worldwide have dealt with these challenges. Here we examine international regulations, as well as laws in the United States, the European Union, and several other countries including Britain, Canada, and Australia in an effort to determine how the world is balancing the threat of online terrorism with the need to safeguard civil rights.

A similar examination of how the Israeli legal system is dealing with this challenge is the focus of Chapter 3. Chapter 4 offers a technical examination of encryption and explains how information is gathered on the Internet. Encryption software is one of the most common and effective means of protection. In the legal sphere, the threat of information warfare demands a reconsideration of the regulation of encryption products. Such products serve the State in securing the information in its possession, but may also serve hostile groups in achieving their aims. The regulation of encryption products is an issue that emphasizes the questions underlying the whole discussion: the balance between security needs and individual rights, the cost of intervention in the marketplace, and, fundamentally, the applicability of traditional legal concepts to the online environment.

Finally, Chapter 5 assesses the law's ability to regulate technology in its efforts to assist law enforcement agencies in the war on terror and offers recommendations for new regulations.

Chapter 1
The Balance Between Security and Civil Rights

As we enter the third millennium, the digital information environment plays a key role in our lives. It is not just a public marketplace or an infinite repository of information. A growing segment of human activity today takes place in that environment: interpersonal communications, civic life and politics, commerce, management and control of essential infrastructure systems, research, and more. However, this arena has also become a battlefront, as the events of September 11, 2001 and their legal aftermath have shown.

In recent years, throughout the democratic world, nations have struggled with adapting rules and concepts that were developed in the context of a concrete, brick and mortar world to a new virtual environment. Initially, the questions dealt with by legislators, courts and researchers mainly concerned commercial contexts, such as adapting intellectual property and privacy laws to the new medium, or criminal contexts, such as gambling and the fight against pedophilia. While these issues are still on the regulator's agenda, today, worldwide attention is being given to a new security threat in the form of global terrorism. Legal systems are being called upon to provide a response to these threats in all areas of life, including the online environment. The fundamental issue – the tension between security needs and civil rights – is not new. A great deal of experience has been amassed in various countries regarding these issues. The question that now arises is whether the existing system of principles and laws, developed on the basis of experience gathered in the concrete world, is applicable to the digital environment.

This chapter argues that the online environment is a significant and relevant arena in the war against terror, maps the field and points to the core difficulties of fighting terror online. First, we identify the terrorist threats, the response of law enforcement agencies and governments and focus on the unique aspects of the online environment. We examine whether this

M. C. Golumbic, *Fighting Terror Online.*
© Springer 2008

environment requires new legal solutions or whether existing solutions are sufficient. Second, we elaborate on three areas of online activity that are particularly acute in the context of fighting terror online, and hence require reexamination: data security, monitoring, and terror propaganda. For each of these, we set out the principles at stake, and address the general framework.

This chapter further demonstrates the need to recognize the complex nature of the digital environment: It is a public facility through which users conduct business activities and engage in political, social and personal interactions. At the same time, however, the online environment is becoming an electronic battlefield in which enforcement agencies are exercising power to address new security threats. The discussion that follows addresses these various elements, and conceptualizes them against the background of the interplay of law, technology, and security.

1.1 Mapping the Threats: Preventing Physical and Virtual Terrorist Attacks

Formulation of an appropriate legal policy at the interface between security, human rights, technology, and economic policy is impossible unless we recognize the security threats faced by states and individuals, the resulting security needs, and existing countermeasures. This section identifies these threats and provides a taxonomy that will assist us later on, when we search for the best response to them.

Discussions of defense strategy often address questions of power buildup, composition of forces, strength in military, economic and moral terms, identification of vulnerabilities, relative and absolute advantages, and threat analysis. Security threats are of two general types. First, is an *existential threat*, namely a threat that may undermine a state or at least lead to heavy loss of life and/or extensive damage to strategic assets and national infrastructure. In general, this type of threat is posed by states with an organized military structure. Nuclear war, for example, is generally viewed as an existential threat by most countries. For small countries such as Israel, an all-out war with enemy states would be considered an existential threat. A second type of security threat is a *nuisance*, which is a threat that may cause loss of life or damage, but not to the extent that it would pose a threat to the existence of the State. Generally, this applies to terrorist acts carried out by non-state organizations (although some are supported by states) with the aim of achieving political goals.

Of course, this is not a simple binary scale: between these two extremes, one might identify threats at various intermediate levels. The terror attacks of September 11, 2001 raised the threat of terror in the international arena from the nuisance level to a level closer to that of an existential threat. The murder of thousands of people within a matter of minutes and the critical damage, both economic and symbolic, to the nerve centers of the international economy and the American defense establishment, were much closer, at least in terms of effect, to the deto-nation of a nuclear bomb, than to any localized terror attack. The danger of biological or chemical terror and the fear that terrorist organizations may gain control of nuclear weapons emphasize the increased importance of the terrorist threat. Furthermore, the distinction between a threat that emanates from an enemy state and its classification as an existential threat, juxtaposed by threats that emanate from non-state organizations, is also blurred. Some terrorist organizations are funded and militarily supported by certain states. This, for example, is the position that the United States State Department holds with regard to Iran and Syria.[1] Accordingly, the importance of the distinction between state-based threats and non-state terror threats, or between existential and nuisance threats, has diminished. This fact takes on renewed significance when we discuss the use of technological tools within the realm of computer and communications systems.

In a personal communication, my colleagues, Michael Birnhack and Niva Elkin-Koren, professors of law and technology at the University of Haifa, noted:

> Another key distinction is between cyber-crime and cyber-terrorism.[2] This distinction is fundamental for designing legal policies that address hostile activities. The distinction between cyber-crime and cyber-terror is based on the aims of the perpetrator. The first term generally relates to "conventional" crime, while the second is associated with activities specifically designed to cause harm to individuals in the interests of making a political statement. Clearly, these are two ends of a spectrum. At one end, we would place a teenage hacker tinkering with the Internet out of curiosity and for enjoy-ment, yet at the same time causing enormous damage (virtual, financial, and

---

[1] See U.S. State Department, 2005 Country Report on Terrorism, Chapter 6 (April 2006), avail-able at http://www.state.gov/s/ct/rls/crt/2005/64337.htm (stating that "Iran and Syria routinely provide unique safe haven, substantial resources and guidance to terrorist organizations.").
[2] See Ariel T. Sobelman, *Is Everyone an Enemy in Cyberspace?* 2(4), Strategic Assessment, (February 2000), available at http://www.tau.ac.il/jcss/sa/v2n4p4.html.

even physical). At the other end of the spectrum is a terrorist who uses the Internet to cause loss of life and property in order to promote his political goals. Between the two lie an infinite number of other situations.[3] It is important to note that the lack of uniform terminology is not only a semantic problem. Labeling an act as "terrorism," particularly on the part of law enforcement agencies, provides the authorities with wider leeway of action. Such labeling also has a symbolic meaning. The willingness of the public and courts to accept a violation of individual rights in the name of preventing terrorism is greater than in the case of conventional crime, even if the methods and countermeasures are the same in both cases.[4] The title of the main legislative response in the United States to the events of September 11 is telling: the USA PATRIOT Act, which is an acronym of Uniting and Strengthening America by Providing Appropriate Tools Required to Intercept and Obstruct Terrorism. Its symbolism is significant.[5] In legal jargon, the distinction between crime and terror may have implications for the weight of the conflicting interests, which is relevant for the constitutional process of balancing.[6]

1.2 Designing Policies to Address New Security Threats

This subsection highlights three main areas of security needs, and explores the main dilemmas and policy considerations they raise. Security needs are discussed here in the context of data security, monitoring of communications, and terrorist propaganda. The next subsection of this chapter will present the other side of the regulatory dilemma: human rights. The discussion is rooted in the context of the unique attributes of the digital environment. This discussion will lay the ground for the legal analysis in Chapter 3.

---

[3] See the Convention on Cyber-Crime, promoted by the Council of Europe, available at http://conventions.coe.int/Treaty/en/Treaties/Html/185.htm.

[4] Richard Forno, *You Say Hacker, The Feds Say Terrorist*, SECURITY FOCUS ONLINE (November 2001), available at http://online.securityfocus.com/columnists/38.

[5] Legal scholar Bruce Ackerman writes that the USA PATRIOT Act "was used as a symbol to reassure the country that Washington was grimly determined to step up and fight against terrorism." See Bruce Ackerman, BEFORE THE NEXT ATTACK: PRESERVING CIVIL LIBERTIES IN AN AGE OF TERRORISM 2 (New Haven, 2006).

[6] The constitutional method of balancing conflicting interest is applied in European law, as well as Israeli law. For discussion of this methodology in general, see Aharon Barak, *A Judge on Judging: The Role of a Supreme Court in a Democracy*, 116 HARV. L. REV. 16 (2002). In the United States the question will be framed as evaluating the "governmental interest" – is it a "pressing need"?

1.2.1 Information Warfare

Information warfare is a broad concept, which also includes cyber-terrorism. A helpful definition is found in the Israeli State Comptroller's Report for 2001 that defines information warfare as "carrying out acts, whose aim is to damage the enemy's computer systems (aggressive information warfare) while defending your own computer systems (defensive information warfare). The most common forms of attack are: theft of data and information (damage to secrecy), and interruptions and destruction of electronic installations (damage to reliability and availability). One of the basic scenarios in aggressive information warfare is an attack against a number of essential computer systems simultaneously."[7]

Attacks may be carried out by a whole spectrum of harmful and destructive programs[8]: viruses, worms, Trojan horses, logic bombs, back doors (trap doors) and "chipping" in hardware components (see the boxes below for descriptions).

Virus: A computer *virus* is a program like any other, but, unlike other programs, computer viruses are designed to copy themselves into other programs. Also, unlike regular programs, the aim of the virus is to damage programs residing on the computer. When the user runs a program infected by a virus, the virus code is also run, launching commands that may damage files on the computer or even delete them.

Worm: A *worm* is an independent program that copies itself from computer to computer across the Internet, often causing overload on the computers through which it passes. However, unlike a virus, it generally does not cause serious damage. In contrast to viruses, worms are not code fragments that attach themselves to or modify existing files. Rather, they are more like stand-alone programs. The first model of a worm was demonstrated as an experiment in early 1988 and caused a furor in the world of computers. Even if the worm itself is not designed to cause damage, the fact that it uses computer resources leads, in the end, to the computer's being slowed down, often negatively impacting the users.[1]

Trojan Horse: A *Trojan horse* is a program whose task is to place itself on a computer, while hiding the fact of its own existence, and operate or allow remote operation of certain actions on the computer. A Trojan horse is not a virus, although it has similar characteristics. Trojan horses are introduced surreptitiously through an

---

(continued)

---

[7] Israel State Comptroller, *Hearchut HaMedinah leAvtahat Sherutim Memuhshavim* [State Preparedness for Protecting Computerized Services], Annual Report 52A for 2001, 275–276 (internal citations omitted).

[8] For further information, see Dorothy Denning & Frank Drake, *A Dialog on Hacking and Security*, in COMPUTERS, ETHICS AND SOCIAL VALUES 120–25 (Deborah G. Johnson & Helen Nissenbaum eds., Englewood Cliffs, NJ, Prentice Hall, 1995).

(continued)

apparently legal file that might arrive through the Internet, email, or on a diskette. These programs install an agent silently, and do nothing to reveal its existence. In fact, the agent does nothing on its own. When we connect to the Internet, our computer is "bombarded" with directed or random probes from penetration programs. These attempts at penetration are carried out through the communications links to the Internet. When such a program finds its agent (server) installed on the target machine, it allows the interloper to send the target computer commands or messages, ranging from "innocent" messages that pop up and surprise users, to commands that reformat the computer's hard drive.

Logic Bomb: The idea behind most *logic bombs* is the misuse of the "Fork" command. This command allows an application to create another copy of itself and to run that copy in parallel. By running a chain of thousands of such commands, the computer's application table fills up, and in the end, the computer grinds to a halt.[2]

Back Doors and **Trap Doors:** *Back doors / trap doors* are loopholes in computer systems deliberately left by developers, technicians or systems managers for later use by them. Sometimes this refers to loopholes in an encryption method. Back doors allow access to the computer system, often without the need for a user name or password.

Chipping: *Chipping* is a term related to the introduction of destructive code into processor chips by the manufacturers. The code will run when a given combination of conditions is met, for example, when a certain signal is received at a particular frequency.

---

[1] For further details, see Peter J. Denning, *The Internet Worm*, AMERICAN SCIENTIST 126–28 (March–April 1989).
[2] On application tables and the original uses for which the Fork command was designed, see Maurice J. Bach, THE DESIGN OF THE UNIX OPERATING SYSTEM 192–200 (New Jersey, Prentice Hall, 1990).

These methods are aimed at a range of targets. Penetration of critical infrastructure can cause damage of various types, from damage to the computer systems themselves (causing mainly economic damage), through the theft of data and its misuse, to the disruption of these systems' activities in ways that cause physical damage in the real world. These actions are aspects of cyber-terrorism. For example, it is possible to destroy key financial systems in the economy or to paralyze the State's supply of electricity, to take over air-traffic control or to paralyze transportation and communication networks. A key vulnerability of Western society in the information age is that of the information systems underlying national infrastructures, including logistics, finance, health, water, electricity, and communications. Such vulnerabilities exist both because of society's heavy reliance on information technology (IT) systems and because of the interconnectedness of those systems through a network that is open to the public.[9] Computer systems are, by their nature, service providers. The more essential a service is to the State's economy and its proper functioning, the more it can be considered a critical infrastructure of strategic importance. By weighing the strategic value of critical infrastructures, we can derive the strategic value of attacking and damaging them.

The response to threats against essential systems can take place on a number of levels. On the practical level, in the United States, there a number of authorities whose task is to protect essential infrastructure in general, and computer systems in particular. Among them are the National Infrastructure Protection Center (NIPC) and the Critical Infrastructure Assurance Office (CIAO). Both have been integrated into the Department of Homeland Security.[10] Discussion of this issue in the United States is open, and there is an ongoing dialogue between the government and the private sector. Various organizations are strongly critical of the Administration's actions in this area. They question the effectiveness of these measures and are concerned about a curtailment of individual rights.[11] A similar dialogue is almost nonexistent in Israel. The 2001 Comptroller's Report is an exception, but even this document conceals more than it reveals. The Report discusses the complexity of defensive information warfare. The Report also stresses the need for a single body to coordinate the issue of securing information in the State's various computerized services on the basis of a system-wide plan.[12]

---

[9] On the vulnerability of the communications infrastructure, see George Smith, *An Electronic Pearl Harbor? Not Likely*, Issues in Science and Technology (1998), available at http://www.nap.edu/issues/15.1/smith.htm. On potential targets for attack, paralysis of websites, worms, attacks on routers, infrastructure attack and combined attacks, see Michael A. Vatis, *Cyber Attacks During the War on Terrorism: A Predictive Analysis (Institute for Security Technology Studies* (Dartmouth College, September 22, 2001), available at http://www.ists.dartmouth.edu/analysis/cyber_a1.pdf. On the risks to critical infrastructures, see General Accounting Office, *Report to the U.S. Senate, Critical Infrastructure Protection – Special Committee on the Year 2000 Technology Problem* (U.S. Senate, October 1999), available at http://www.gao.gov/archive/2000/ai00001.pdf.

[10] See http://www.dhs.gov/.

[11] *See* EPIC (Electronic Privacy Information Center) available at http://www.epic.org/; ACLU (American Civil Liberties Union), available at http://www.aclu.org/.

[12] According to the Israeli State Comptroller, defensive information warfare is built on a number of different levels: deterrence, warning, protection, identification and prevention of future attack, response at the level that has been attacked, and response at the national level (preparation of the State to cope in the absence of available computer systems in the accepted form, and the response of the State to aggressive information warfare from the outside). Based on this definition, the Comptroller raises a number of fundamental questions that require a response: Who and what to protect? From what and from whom? Who will do the defending? How is the

One of the most common and effective means of protection is the use of encryption software. In the legal sphere, the threat of information warfare demands a reconsideration of the regulation of encryption products. Such products serve the State in securing the information in its possession, but may also serve hostile groups in achieving their aims. The regulation of encryption products is an issue that emphasizes the questions that underlie the whole discussion: the balance between security needs and individual rights, the cost of intervention in the marketplace, and, fundamentally, the applicability of traditional legal concepts to the online environment. These issues involving encryption will be dealt with more fully in the following subsection.

1.2.2 Data Security

Essential government systems, as well as essential civilian systems, require maximal protection. Some threats against critical infrastructure can be addressed by data security strategies. Encryption is also essential for protecting diplomatic and military communications, national defense secrets and other forms of sensitive data.

Encryption is always vulnerable to deciphering attempts, which require computing power. Cyber-terrorism that targets critical infrastructure requires significant computational power in order to crack complex encryption that protects information systems.

The dissemination of supercomputers capable of carrying out computations of this nature was therefore restricted by regulation. Today, however, distributed computing, where a task is allocated among many computers or clusters of computers, and is conducted in parallel, approaches the computing power of some supercomputers. Distributed computing thus enables collaborating individuals to utilize computer power that was once the sole province of states and multinational corporations.

Encryption is not only a means for securing critical infrastructure but also for protecting sensitive government information. Yet, the demand for effective encryption products is not in any way purely governmental.

---

defense accomplished and to what degree? In view of the mutual dependence between service systems, it is not enough for each body to plan independently, as has been the case to date. Instead, there is a need for an overall systemic view of planning. See http://www.mevaker.gov.il (Document 52a)[Hebrew].

Players in the free market often must use encryption to protect their own information and to engage in e-commerce. Encryption of business information might also be considered a "reasonable measure" for protecting a trade secret, under trade secret law, or enabling vendors to protect the privacy of their customers.[13]

Some defense and security bodies develop their own encryption products, for their own use, so there is no need for or difficulty in limiting the dissemination of these encryption products. It is not in the organizations' interest to disseminate the encryption products, and their ownership enables them to control the relevant cryptographic knowledge about how the products work. In such cases, however, the data security problem and the control of encryption products may be compromised by information drift, when, for example, an employee leaves the agency for the private sector. The use of restrictive contractual provisions in the employment contract, and the enforcement of proprietary protections such as trade secrets and prohibitions against spying with criminal sanctions, rather than through direct intervention in the encryption market, is the preferred strategy for dealing with this issue. This leads us to the topic of encryption products that are produced in the free, private market, for use by the general public.

We have addressed the governmental security need to regulate encryption products; however, this is only one part of the picture. The other part complicates the issue of regulation to a far greater degree. Encryption can also be used by hostile groups to coordinate activities and promote their goals. The widespread availability of encryption means that investigators encounter difficulties in accessing information necessary for law enforcement and security purposes. The stronger the encryption products are, the more difficult it is for law enforcement agencies to gather information about the terrorists and their plans.

From a legal perspective, it is necessary to reconsider the regulation of encryption. The regulation of encryption brings with it conflicting policy objectives, such as national security and law enforcement on the one hand, and civil liberties, R&D, and economic competitiveness on the other.

Encryption policy has already been the subject of a bitter debate between the U.S. government and the American information industries. The question is whether increasing security threats and the use of the

---

[13] See Uniform Trade Secrets Act, Drafted by the National Conference of Commissioners on Uniform State Laws, as amended 1985.

Internet for hostile purposes requires any adjustment to encryption policies. The regulation of encryption is an issue that reflects the fundamental questions related to fighting terror online: How do we balance security needs and individual rights? How do we minimize the negative cost of government intervention on research and development and on the marketplace? Finally, how do we apply traditional legal checks and balances to the online environment?

We now turn to discuss another aspect of security strategy: monitoring. Following this discussion, we will return to the policy considerations of regulating encryption when security needs themselves pull in opposite directions.

1.2.3 Gathering Information and Surveillance

In recent years, the Internet has become a primary medium for communication and information management. Its end-to-end (e2e) structure enables the implementation and constant change of endless applications, many of which serve as communication devices for sending and receiving messages between different parties, as well as for managing information efficiently and interactively. The Internet allows for the transfer of complex messages in various formats. It enables not only asynchronous exchange by email, but also synchronous chat in real-time, speech (VoIP), transmission of photographs and video, satellite images, as well as software and other applications. This type of network design allows ordinary citizens to participate actively in the public sphere and opens up new opportunities to further democratic values. Yet, from the point of view of fighting terror, this wealth of information is also one of the primary drawbacks of the Internet, making it increasingly difficult to extract valuable information from the vast amount of data available online. Indeed, the online environment as a surveillance arena poses new challenges for intelligence efforts. On the one hand, online activities leave digital tracks, which can be monitored and traced. On the other hand, *information smog* makes it easier to hide hostile activities. Thus, the great technological developments of the information age have had a major influence on the thought processes and work methods of intelligence organizations worldwide.

The classical intelligence source was *human intelligence*, namely, intelligence derived from human sources, such as spies, agents, collaborators, and interrogation of captives.[14] Although human intelligence was once the exclusive and best source of intelligence information, it is now accompanied by non-human sources. Intelligence organizations now routinely obtain information through various technological means, primarily through *signal intelligence*.[15] Signal intelligence refers to communications intelligence, electronic intelligence, and technological intelligence. Specifically, signal intelligence refers to intelligence produced by listening to and decrypting signals primarily through the wiretapping of telephone, cellular, and fax communications and now, digital communications, and through the intercepting and monitoring of Internet communications of various kinds, including Internet telephony (VoIP). These signals can be derived from electromagnetic waves or fiber-optic transmissions, as well as from data and Internet communications, such as email, instant messages, and site infrastructures. Due to its centrality as a means of communication, the Internet has thus become an important source for obtaining intelligence information. Signal intelligence now constitutes a widespread and high-quality intelligence tool, in particular among the leading intelligence organizations in the world.[16] In the past, the collection of intelligence material required a hefty investment in resources and manpower. Today, electronic monitoring techniques employed on a global web, using powerful computers, enable the efficient collection of such material.

In this context, we need to distinguish between defensive intelligence measures and offensive measures. Here we recognize a continuum rather than a dichotomy. Defensive measures aim at gathering information about the terrorist activities, in addition to undertaking means of data security, discussed in the previous subsection. Offensive measures include the location and apprehension of attackers and direct strikes against them, as well as the utilization of computer networks as an offensive weapon. In the discussion that follows here, we focus on the defensive, information-gathering task of security agencies.

A central technological point in our discussion is that any action in a digital web leaves digital tracks. The routine operations of sending

---

[14] See Robert H. Kupperman & M. Trent Darrell, TERRORISM: THREAT, REALITY, RESPONSE (Stanford, CA, Hoover Institution Press, 1979).

[15] See the explanation offered by the National Security Agency (NSA), available at http://www.nsa.gov/sigint/. See also Michael Wilson, *Considering the Net as an Intelligence Tool* (1996–2002), available at http://www.metatempo.com/NetIntelligence.pdf.

[16] See Arthur S. Hulnick, KEEPING US SAFE: SECRET INTELLIGENCE AND HOMELAND SECURITY 66–72 (Westport, CT, 2004).

electronic mail, surfing and downloading files are recorded in various files on the personal computer (PC) and the servers involved in the communications. For instance, unlike a telephone call that is ephemeral and remains only in space and in the memory of the speakers (unless recorded or intercepted at real-time), an Internet chat leaves behind a log of the chat, indicating not only what Internet Protocol (IP) address was connected to what other IP address, the duration of the chat and comparable "external" details about the exchange, but also the contents of the exchange. Once the IP addresses are recorded, they can be easily deciphered and reverse engineered to trace their Internet Service Providers (ISPs). With the assistance (either willing or judicially mandated) of these ISPs, the computer from which the chat took place can be identified. The last action to be taken is to establish who used the computer. This goal might be easy to accomplish when the computer is located in a home, but more difficult if it is located in an Internet café or public library, for instance, and particularly difficult if a wireless connection was used. Although tracing the speakers requires several technological and perhaps legal steps, it is not a complex process. Thus, the wealth of information and level of detail available from monitoring the Internet is clearly unprecedented.

This emphasis on using technological intelligence comes in response to a parallel shift among the intelligence targets as well. They, too, have evolved in their communication techniques and now make use of the latest technology. Alongside the possibility of hostile elements using the digital environment as a weapon (direct use) to cause damage, the Internet also serves as a communications medium through which these hostile forces can maintain contact among themselves, as well as a means for collecting information (indirect use).

Thus, alongside legal activity on the Web (such as daily communication, e-commerce, education and academic research), the Internet also serves as a communications means for intelligence targets of various kinds, from criminal agencies to terror organizations. This dual use of the Internet means that terrorists act within a civil environment, and targeting the terrorists might negatively affect the benign users. In other words, the main difficulty in executing intelligence in this environment is that the Internet is an open, global form of communication. For this reason, monitoring terrorist activity on the Internet, with the intention of nipping it in the bud, may result in violating the privacy of others and limiting their freedom of expression. It should be apparent that the means of information collection in the Internet environment are highly invasive. Internet communications are based on the distribution of data to packets sent by the sending computer and routed in the Web separately, until finally they are collected and arranged by the receiving computer. In these circumstances, transmissions of intelligence targets are likely to be swallowed up in innocent transmissions. The problem is acute when the target is not specified in advance and needs to be located within a huge civilian environment. Therefore, the monitoring of the Internet may inevitably involve the monitoring and collection of extensive material on people who are entirely innocent. Consequently, the advantages of gathering intelligence information by monitoring the Internet do come with a major disadvantage: the threat to individual liberty.

Given the unique characteristics of the Internet, it may be necessary to reexamine the existing regulations regarding the checks and balances between meeting security needs and protecting the rights of the individual. Legislation in democratic regimes must strike a balance between serving the intelligence needs of various law enforcement agencies and safeguarding the rights of the individual. The application of the existing checks and balances developed in the offline environment to the digital environment calls for adjustments, in line with the new threats to individual rights. Thus far, it seems that the checks and balances have tilted in the direction of stronger security measures, often at the expense of civil liberties and the rights of citizens.[17] Also worth considering is the fact that many intelligence operations are apt to be carried out on the equipment and servers of commercial agencies. Thus, the cooperation of these agencies (voluntary or judicially or otherwise required) is unavoidable.[18]

To summarize, terrorists use the Internet as a communications tool, and thus are targets for new forms of intelligence, i.e., signal intelligence. The terrorist activity takes place in a civilian environment, and hence, law enforcement agencies face a new challenge, as their targets blend in with legitimate activities in an environment that provides unprecedented advantages. We have the technical capability to trace users. The question, therefore, becomes one of policy. Are we willing to surrender some of our privacy and freedom of expression in order to prevent terrorism? While the law is familiar with such conflicts in the offline context, we have yet to determine whether the old responses to this conflict fit the online environment.

---

[17] Several commentators argue that the checks and balances applied in the offline world have also gone astray. *See e.g.*, Ackerman, *supra* note 5.

[18] For a critical discussion of the cooperation of law enforcement agencies and private entities, see Michael D. Birnhack & Niva Elkin-Koren, *The Invisible Handshake: The Reemergence of the State in the Digital Environment*, 8 VA. J. OF L. & TECH. 6 (2003).

1.2.4 Regulation of Encryption Products

Thus far, we have discussed two main security needs: protecting the data held by governmental and other critical infrastructure agencies on the one hand and the need to utilize signal intelligence to gather information about terrorists and terror activities on the other. Each of these needs raises difficulties, but at one point, the two security needs conflict directly with one another. That area is in the regulation of encryption.

Until the late 1990s and early 2000s, a number of countries, including the United States and Israel, imposed various kinds of regulation of encryption products. However, over the years, these restrictive policies have been relaxed, and replaced by more moderate supervisory policies.[19] Are these regulations justified?

In the past, security forces throughout the world have encountered attempts by terrorist organizations and other hostile groups to conceal their activities by means of encryption. In 1998, the Director of the FBI testified before the Senate Select Committee on Intelligence and noted the use of encryption by the spy, Aldrich Ames, who was asked by his Soviet handlers to encrypt the material that he transmitted to them.[20] Similarly, the plot by Ramzi Yousef and other terrorists to blow up eleven American airliners in the Far East also relied on encrypted materials. Yousef's laptop computer, which was seized in Manila, contained encrypted files relating to the terrorist plot.[21]

Intelligence is a complex art, and the volume of communications passing through modern communications channels has become a challenge for intelligence agencies with limited resources. It is therefore necessary to map information flows and to focus on intercepting the most important channels. Doing so allows intelligence services to focus their attention on the most important messages passing through the various channels. It is only after this stage that the more familiar part of the intelligence process takes place. For this purpose, the message has to be stripped of its protective mechanisms (this generally means decryption) before any intelligence assessment of its nature and content can take place. Those who think in terms of the vulnerability of communication from a security point of view see encryption as the main obstacle for intelligence. By

---

[19] We will return to the legal analysis of encryption regulation in Chapter 5.

[20] See the statement of the Director of the FBI, Louis J. Freeh, before the Senate Select Committee on Intelligence, *Threats to U.S. National Security* (1998), available at http://www.fas.org/irp/congress/1998_hr/s980128f.htm.

[21] *Id.*

extension, an enemy who is aware of the way in which his communications are being used may try to modify these channels in order to make their use more difficult.[22] Encryption is one of the most effective means of achieving this goal.

Thus, encryption technology can be used by both sides. It provides reasonably strong protection for stored data and for communication over digital networks. In determining the best policy in the field, we face the need to protect data held by the government, including the security agencies themselves, as well as other critical infrastructure such as hospitals, transportation services, food supplies, and communications networks (collectively, *protection needs*). On the other hand, we have the security need to obtain information of defense value held by the enemy (*monitoring needs*). Data security needs pull in the direction of encouraging a software market without state interference, while monitoring needs pull in the opposite direction of imposing limitations on the software market in order to prevent terrorists from using encryption products. Furthermore, regulation today faces a practical difficulty that cannot be overlooked: strong encryption products are readily available on the open market.

In addition to security needs, there are other considerations that should not be disregarded. Intervention in the marketplace for encryption technologies changes the incentive scheme of the players in the market. In as much as software is considered a form of expression, interference in the marketplace also limits freedom of expression, and restricts the ability of citizens to communicate securely and privately. Such interference might also interfere with the freedom to engage in one's occupation and possibly with property rights. A practical policy needs to fulfill both types of security needs (protection and monitoring), while attempting to limit the violation of human rights and minimize intervention in the free market.

An argument in favor of the regulation of encryption technology in general and the refusal to grant permits for the use of reasonably strong encryption in particular, would keep such technology out of the hands of those targeted by intelligence services. In parallel, an orderly system of registration and licensing would provide information about and control over the uses of encryption.

In spite of the security needs, it appears at first glance that technology has already won. Encryption technology exists in the open market and is available to anyone who wants it, in shops and on the Internet, either at

---

[22] See CODES, KEYS AND CONFLICTS: ISSUES IN U.S. CRYPTO POLICY (ACM, US Public Policy Committee 1994).

a reasonable price or for free. In view of the fact that national borders no longer pose any real obstacle and that the digital environment can easily overcome any obstacles, the question then arises: Is there indeed any reason for regulation?

A positive answer cites two reasons: moral and practical. First, even if total control of the distribution of encryption products and preventing terrorists from acquiring them is difficult – even perhaps doomed to failure – this in itself does not justify giving up.[23] In dealing with terrorism, it may be useful for security agencies to know which technology is in the hands of terrorists. Such information can make it somewhat easier to thwart terrorism. In addition, where the State has a back door, that is, a super-key that allows it to penetrate the encryption, its access to terrorist information will be greatly increased. The use of backdoors is highly controversial, but where it exists, it enables better response to encryption by the targets. Second, in order to use an encryption product in the optimal manner, technical support from the developer is usually necessary. Regulation of encryption products might render it harder for a terrorist to use that particular encryption product.

Therefore, we believe that security concerns are valid, despite the easy availability of strong encryption products on the open market. However, this in itself does not mean that all regulation is permitted. Security concerns need to be balanced with other considerations.

1.2.5 Terror Propaganda

Terrorists have a continuous and complex relationship with traditional mass media. Terror in itself is an act of propaganda, as often seeking to garner public and international attention and support as to inflict actual harm. Terrorists also try to deliver their message through words, photographs and videos, hereinafter referred to as *terror propaganda*. The expansion of public discourse from newspapers and electronic mass media to the online environment transforms the way in which we communicate with one another. This change alters who defines what is on the public agenda, how opinions are formulated and how citizens are informed. Terrorist propaganda is being affected by this transformation too. This subsection explores the changes that result from the shift of terrorist

---

[23] For an argument in a similar vein, see CODES, KEYS AND CONFLICTS, id.

communicative activity from the offline media to the online environment. We discuss the terrorists' use of the media, evaluate the differences between the offline and online worlds, and query the role of law. Can the law do anything to address this kind of terrorist activity? What are the ramifications of various policy choices? The legal questions that are most likely to arise in this context are how to differentiate illicit terrorist communications from legitimate speech, and how to evaluate the role that intermediaries play in an effort to determine whether imposing liability on them is both effective in blocking terror and not unduly harmful to their civil liberties.

Terror and propaganda. Terrorism itself is a type of communication, namely, the transmission of a message. However, it is a communication that is delivered by actions rather than by words. In this sense, terror in itself constitutes propaganda. Yet, the main goal of any terrorist activity is to terrorize by causing harm in the real world, and communicative consequences are of indirect nature. Accordingly, we refer to terrorist activities as *indirect propaganda* and to communicative efforts by the terrorists as *direct propaganda.* Groups and organizations that carry out violent acts in order to further their political objectives intimidate through communication. Terrorist organizations depend on the publicity accorded them, without which they cannot exist. In this sense, a symbiotic relationship exists between terror and the media,[24] insofar as without the publicity and advertising provided to terrorist organizations by the media, their struggle would have no value. British Prime Minister Margaret Thatcher aptly commented that terrorist organizations hunger for the "oxygen of publicity."[25] Mass media channels competing for viewers may play into the hands of the terrorist organizations, which provide abundant drama, and are liable to disseminate their propaganda unknowingly and unwillingly. Thus, a vicious cycle is created: The more media coverage is given to terrorist organizations, the greater is the potential for acts of terror. This cycle naturally raises questions about the scope and nature of media coverage of terror attacks.

---

[24] See Paul Wilkinson, *The Media and Terror: A Reassessment*, 9 TERRORISM AND POLITICAL VIOLENCE 51–65 (1997) (hereafter: Wilkinson). For a contrasting approach, see Michel Wieviorka, THE MAKING OF TERRORISM (Chicago, University of Chicago Press, 1993) (rejecting the claim that a symbiotic relationship exists between the media and the terrorist organizations).

[25] "We must try to find ways to starve the terrorist and the hijacker of the oxygen of publicity on which they depend." Speech by Margaret Thatcher to the American Bar Association, July 15, 1985, available at http://www.margaretthatcher.org/speeches/displaydocument.asp?docid=106096.

Propaganda terror (ab)uses the freedom of speech and of the press enjoyed by the mass media to transmit its harmful messages. The free communications in democratic societies are extremely vulnerable to exploitation and manipulation by terrorist organizations as an effective and convenient tool in their attack on democratic values. Propaganda terror uses democratic values and freedom of speech to trap government authorities, so that they either grow accustomed to the propaganda published or resort to censuring communications, thereby incurring public criticism.[26] However, it should be clear that this problem should be addressed by the media itself, not by the government. Any governmental intervention would be unconstitutional censorship, and an abridgment of the freedom of the press.

Direct propaganda also constitutes a major part of the activity of terrorist organizations. Terror propaganda is an attempt to create a reality that brings the terrorist's cause to the forefront. Such psychological warfare attacks the adversary's credo, outlook, and values.[27] For psychological warfare to succeed, it is necessary to know and understand the opinions and values "professed by the enemy."[28]

Willkinson helpfully identifies four main objectives of the terrorist organizations' use of propaganda. The first is sowing fear and terror in the "target group." The rationale is that if the enemy is afraid, it will be more easily defeated. Professor Bruce Ackerman made a similar argument, stating that, "by assaulting our confident sense of sovereignty, they [Al-Qaeda] want us to destroy ourselves, throwing away our priceless heritage of liberal democracy in a panic cycle leading to authoritarianism."[29] Second, terrorists hope to garner extensive support for their struggle in the local population and in the court of world opinion by justifying their goals and describing their inevitable victory. Third, the terrorists distort government responses, for instance by representing government actions against terrorists as tyrannical and ineffective. Finally, the terrorists hope to mobilize activists for participation in information campaigns, for fundraising, and for recruiting supporters.

---

[26] Yariv Tsfati & Gabriel Weimann, *Terror be-Internet* (Online terror), 4 POLITIKA, 46–47 (2000) [Hebrew]

[27] Sherry Goldstein-Ferber, *Lohma Psichologit be-Eidan Hahartaah Hasheni* (Psychological warfare in the Second Age of Deterrence, 378–79 MAARAKHOT 2, 3 (2001) [Hebrew].

[28] John Elliston, *Psywar Terror Tactics* (1996), available at http://www.parascope.com/ds/1096/psy.htm.

[29] Ackerman, *supra* note 5, at 56.

At the information level, a distinction should be made between the types of propaganda directed at different target populations. The propaganda of the terrorist organizations is directed at potential supporters, within the terrorists' local territory or their targeted territory, and at the international community. The contents of the propaganda will be influenced and shaped by the specific target population. In this context, it is useful to distinguish between hard and soft propaganda.[30] Hard propaganda refers to creating negative opinions and causing alienation between the public and the State. Terrorist organizations accomplish this goal by presenting their "opponents" as the personification of evil and claiming that because the enemy is so corrupt, the terrorists are obligated to annihilate it. The websites of Hezbollah and Hamas, for instance, focus on presenting Israeli military activity as terrorist activity. Presenting the enemy in this way is designed to justify the use of violence and the harming of innocents. Similarly, the website of the Colombian National Liberation Army indicates that the violence carried out by the organization is a result, rather than a cause, of the violence prevailing in the world.[31]

Soft propaganda refers to creating a positive opinion about and support for the terrorist organization leading the struggle.[32] Here the object is to encourage people to support the organization and even to join it by persuading people, young people in particular, to assume the values of the organization, to condone its methods of operation, and to identify with its ideology. For the most part, the terrorist organizations emphasize the justice of their objectives, which are based generally on some ideology. They do not present themselves as terrorists carrying out acts of terror, but as freedom fighters with justified goals and means. Terrorist organizations generally play down their own violent activity and accuse their adversaries of murder and genocide. The terrorist organizations present themselves as innocents whose freedom of speech is curtailed and whose supporters are persecuted by the authorities. Their objective is to undermine the legitimacy of the existing government and to place all the blame for the use of violence on their opponents – all as part of their psychological warfare.

Another propaganda mechanism used by terrorist organizations to create positive opinions about themselves is the rhetoric of peace and nonviolence. Despite the fact that these are, in fact, violent organizations, most claim that they seek peaceful solutions. They argue that in order to

---

[30] B. Raman, *Psychological Warfare (Psywar) in the New Millennium* (1999), available at http://www.saag.org/papers/paper39.html (hereafter: Raman).

[31] See Tsfati & Weimann, *supra* note 26, at 45–57

[32] See Raman, *supra* note 30.

achieve peace and justice, they have no other choice but to use violence. The dissemination of such propaganda relies extensively on attention from journalists, authors, broadcast and publishing media, and most recently, the Internet.

Propaganda terror defined. Thus far, we have examined direct and indirect terror propaganda, the various audiences that the terrorists approach, and the various kinds of messages – soft or hard – that they deliver. However, we need to fine-tune the definition of propaganda terror and differentiate it from other forms of communications, either legitimate or illicit. Here we use the term *propaganda terror* to refer to the practices of disseminating disinformation, of misusing accurate information through digital media, namely the Internet, with its numerous communicative applications, when these activities are aimed at the general public, potential supporters and those already committed to the terrorist agenda. All of these practices serve the purpose of furthering the terrorists' political agenda, as well as their destructive agenda in general.

In this discussion, we will leave aside one-to-one applications, such as email, direct chats, instant messaging and Internet telephony. These forms of communication are less likely to include propaganda, and are more likely to raise other security concerns and hence, other legal challenges. We have addressed these issues in the previous discussion of monitoring. Accordingly, here we address communication in the form of one-to-many, which is similar in structure to the traditional mass media, but differs in many other aspects.

From mass media to digital media. In the offline environment, terrorists have a difficult time conveying their messages. As long as they do not own a public means of communication such as a radio or television station, they must use the conventional, legal media whose editors usually block these kinds of messages. As long as the terrorists wish to operate from within the country they target, the offline world makes it almost impossible for them to do so. In other words, Al-Qaeda could not buy airtime on NBC to broadcast a commercial advocating their cause. However, the online environment enables the terrorists to reach individuals and communities by operating from another country, without the need to rely on any local intermediary. Al-Qaeda can operate a web site from Iran, for example. Can any policy effectively fight terror propaganda?

Several characteristics of the digital medium make it unique. Those presented below do not constitute an exhaustive list, but reflect special aspects of the digital medium. Despite some overlap between them, they should, in any case, be viewed as a whole. These unique characteristics include the independence of the terrorists in executing communications, the ease of accessibility to their audience, the interactive nature of the message, and their use of a global network. All of these features enhance the efficacy of their communications and their appearance of legitimacy.

The first characteristic of the Internet relevant to our discussion is that it enables the terrorists to communicate directly with their potential audiences. Unlike advertising in the mass media, which is centrally managed by publishers who use editing and content control mechanisms, almost anyone can express himself on the Internet (leaving aside the digital divide, which should be irrelevant to the terrorist). Online, the terrorist organization has free reign. It can use general systems, open to the public, such as platforms that host web sites, blogs, forums and similar applications. The direct terrorist communication is not subject to any pre-screening, private censorship or external editorial judgment.

The second characteristic is the accessibility and availability of Internet communication channels to the terrorists. In his frightening new book "Terror on the Internet: The New Arena, the New Challenges", Gabriel Weimann, gives an account of how terrorists use the Internet to carry out their deadly plans everyday[33]. Weimann reports the number of websites operated by suspected terrorist organizations has exploded from 12 in 1998 to more than 4,800 today. Internet propaganda can be conducted and disseminated at relatively low cost. The availability of many free and open platforms such as blogs and forums obliterates the need for technological sophistication. Furthermore, use of these mechanisms is very inexpensive. For example, creating and maintaining a web site is far less costly than buying commercial space in the old media.

The third feature is interactivity. Although we have defined the terror propaganda as a one-to-many format, the Internet, unlike conventional media, allows interactive communications between the terrorist organization and users. The terrorist organization, therefore, has an effective means of contacting activists and managing their activities. For instance, in addition to the propaganda published on the actual website, many terrorist sites offer various services, such as the purchase of books, videotapes, audiotapes, stickers, T-shirts, and emblems of the organization.[34] Such activity on a massive scale, with relatively little cost and easy availability, is not possible in traditional mass media.

---

[33] Gabriel Weimann, TERROR ON THE INTERNET: THE NEW ARENA, THE NEW CHALLENGES (Washington, DC, United States Institute of Peace, 2006).
[34] Tsafti & Weimann, *supra* note 26, at 53.

The final factor is the ability of the terrorist to target the message to a specific audience, customize it to fit the needs of the organization relative to a specific group and even personalize the message. Psychological warfare that uses conventional mass media typically targets the general public or an unspecified group of people. The Internet, on the other hand, makes it possible to select a small target population out of the community and to direct the propaganda only to this population. Different messages can be customized for different communities (world opinion, potential members of the organization, etc.) Therefore, the use of the Internet is likely to be more effective from the terrorist's viewpoint. However, despite the fact that the Internet is accessible at a low cost to almost any speaker without censorship, filtering or editing, it does have certain disadvantages for the terrorists. Rather than taking center stage as its message might if it were delivered through the mass media, terrorist propaganda messages are likely to be swallowed up in the *data smog*[35] and get lost in the overload of information. This prospect is not a fatal factor as far as the terrorists are concerned, because there are various means available to overcome the problem, such as search engines and links among terrorist organizations. Furthermore, Internet communications are not exclusive. In order to gain broader public exposure, terrorist organizations often use acts of terror as a way to transmit their message through the mass media.

Finally, the globalization of the network is an important feature of the online environment that makes it easier for terrorists to use the Internet for their propaganda purposes. The Internet is accessible to hundreds of millions around the world, and enables speakers to use it from anywhere around the globe. A terrorist can act from Iran, North Korea, Syria and other countries, including those that support terror against other countries. This capability enables terrorists to reach other public groups outside the region in which they operate, offering them tremendous informational and operational advantages for recruiting and activating supporters outside territorial borders.

The cumulative impact of these features is that it is easy and highly effective for terrorists to conduct terror propaganda in the digital environment, allowing them to bypass traditional gatekeepers, and act beyond the reach of traditional law enforcement.[36]

---

[35] *See* David Shenk, DATA SMOG: SURVIVING THE INFORMATION GLUT (New York, Harper Collins, 1997).

[36] One commentator aptly concluded that the Internet is an optimal arena for terrorists. See Shaul Shay, *The Radical Islam and the Cyber Jihad*, in FIGHTING TERROR IN CYBERSPACE 29, 32 (Mark Last & Abraham Kandel, eds., World Scientific Publishing, 2005). *See also* Abraham R.

The policy dilemma. Acts of terror and terror propaganda both pre-date the digital era. The legal problems that arise in connection with the issues of incitement, sedition, hostile propaganda, and hate speech have been dealt with in depth by Western democracies in the pre-digital envi-ronment. Within that framework, a series of constitutional balances has been established to guide both the executive branch and the courts. These balances attempt to find the golden mean between security needs and free-dom of the press and freedom of expression.

Assuming that the offline balance is satisfactory, can the existing checks and balances be sustained in the digital environment? The discus-sion above reveals some of the difficulties in regulating terrorists' propa-ganda. First, it might be difficult in some cases to distinguish legitimate political speech from terrorist activity, particularly when the terrorists disguise their activities and hide behind other seemingly benign speakers. Second, even after the first problem is resolved, and law enforcement agencies are confident of the terrorist source of the propaganda and even have judicial approval for pursuing them, they may find that they are unable to enforce existing laws because the terrorists are outside their jurisdiction. A possible option is to turn to an intermediary, who is between, technologically speaking, the terrorist and the users, whether the general public or active supporters of the terrorist organization. These are the ISPs. However, imposing law enforcement duties on ISPs raises a host of legal questions, to which we turn later on.

1.3 Preserving Civil Liberties

Prevention and enforcement systems are designed to safeguard the public interest and, more importantly, public order. As understood today, govern-ment authorities are entrusted with protecting the public interest through various systems for identification, interception and monitoring of infor-mation. These measures are in place to prevent activities that conflict with the public interest, including acts of terror. The main danger in the oper-ation of monitoring and information collection systems is that they may infringe on the rights of the individual, in particular the rights to privacy and freedom of speech.

Wagner, *Terrorism and the Internet: Use and Abuse*, in the same volume, 7–10 (discussing the advantages of the Internet for terrorists).

1.3.1 The Right to Privacy

The advanced technology available in the Information Age has brought the discussion of the right to privacy into new arenas. Violations of a person's privacy are no longer limited to conducting a physical search in the home. Today, our privacy is affected by the click of a mouse or as privacy expert Roger Clarke defined it, dataveillance.[37] There are also cases in which the government asks to set up permanent or temporary wiretapping in the name of the public interest. Such an action might require the assistance of a private entity that is an intermediary, and thus a technological bottleneck, located in a convenient position to collect and examine data. Assuming that these means do serve the public interest, the policy dilemma concerns the violations of the privacy of the innocent people who had the misfortune of being in the path of the government in its search for relevant information. This section begins with a short overview of the legal right to privacy, continues by addressing the subject of information privacy, and then turns to digital privacy.

The right to be let alone. The roots of the right to privacy go back to early human history, with clear references found in the Bible, Greek mythology, and ancient China. However, it was not until 1890, when Samuel Warren and Louis Brandeis published one of the most influential law review articles ever written, that privacy was recognized as a legal right. In *The Right to Privacy*, Warren and Brandeis defined it as "the right to be let alone."[38] Warren and Brandeis argued that while many existing legal concepts protect, *inter alia*, privacy interests, such as copyright law, property law and other legal interests, the right to privacy needs to be acknowledged as a separate and independent right. This argument was sufficient to establish the right as a legal concept in U.S. law. However, while the phrase suggested by Warren and Brandeis does capture much of the current legal understanding of the right to privacy, the right remains fuzzy, and the concept of privacy remains elusive. The difficulty in defining the right to privacy is well reflected in its designation as "an individual

---

[37] Clarke's definition of dataveillance is, "the systematic use of personal data systems in the investigation or monitoring of the actions or communications of one or more persons." See Roger Clarke, *Introduction to Dataveillance and Information Privacy, and Definitions of Terms*, (1997, 2006), available at http://www.anu.edu.au/people/Roger.Clarke/DV/Intro.html. *See also* David Lyon, Surveillance Society: Monitoring Everyday Life (Open University Press 2001).
[38] *See* Samuel D. Warren & Louis D. Brandeis, *The Right to Privacy*, 4 Harv. L. Rev. 193 (1890).

right that is self-evident until someone takes it away."[39] The Warren and Brandeis description provides one a sense of what privacy is, but it does not define what privacy is and does not capture other aspects of the right. One of the aspects that is not intuitively covered by this term is privacy in information, or data protection, which is the term applied by the European Union.

Over the years, numerous attempts have been made to define privacy and the right to privacy.[40] In 1960, Dean William Prosser surveyed the use of the right to privacy in U.S. case law since the 1890 publication of Warren and Brandeis' article, and argued that this right is in fact made up of four different torts: intrusion upon the seclusion of another; appropriation of the other's name or likeness; publishing of personal information; and publicity that places a person in a false light.[41] Although Prosser modestly described his project as a descriptive one, his classification turned out to be an influential one and was later adopted by the Restatement (Second) on Torts, as a reflection of the law of privacy, thus adding to Prosser's classification a normative power.[42]

However, the classification does not provide us with a justification for, explanation of, or guidance in this area. Why do we protect the interest individuals have in these situations, and why are other situations not similarly protected? Further literature, more philosophical in nature, attempted to fill the gaps. An influential analysis by Professor Ruth Gavison defines privacy in terms of access, namely, as "a limitation of others' access to an individual."[43] In this sense, a loss of privacy occurs when others have information about the individual, when they draw attention to him or her, or when they receive access to him or her.[44]

An intuitive and influential sociological definition of privacy applies terms of control. Alan Westin defines privacy as "the claims of individuals, groups, or institutions to determine for themselves when, how and

---

[39] David H. Flaherty, *On the Utility of Constitutional Rights to Privacy and Data Protection*, 41 CASE WESTERN RESERVE L. REV. 831–55 (1991).

[40] On the vagueness of the definitions, see Gregory J. Walters, HUMAN RIGHTS IN THE INFORMATION AGE A PHILOSOPHICAL ANALYSIS (London, University of Toronto Press, 2003). See also the articles in PHILOSOPHICAL DIMENSIONS OF PRIVACY: AN ANTHOLOGY (Ferdinand D. Schoeman ed., Cambridge, Cambridge University Press, 1984).

[41] See William Prosser, *Privacy*, 48 CAL. L. REV. 383–423 (1960).

[42] Restatement (Second) of Torts § 652A (1976).

[43] Ruth Gavison, *Privacy and the Limits of Law*, 89 YALE L.J. 421, 428 (1980). Accessibility, in Gavison's opinion, is based on three elements: secrecy, anonymity and solitude.

[44] Irwin Altman, *Privacy Regulations: Culturally Universal or Culturally Specific?* 33 J. OF SOC. 67 (1977); Anita L. Allen, UNEASY ACCESS 3 (1988).

to what extent information about them is communicated to others."[45] If in the past privacy concerned control in the individual-intimate space – a man's home is his castle (and in the past, this was clearly a masculine statement) – then in the modern age, this concept has been expanded and now applies to control of other aspects of the individual. Contemporary concepts of privacy deal not only with a person's control of his or her physical private space, but also with control of his or her intimate decisions[46] and with control of the knowledge of his or her personal affairs.

Information privacy / data protection. These classifications and definitions of privacy and other attempts to explain it, such as on the basis of the need for intimacy,[47] or protection against a panoptic gaze,[48] capture some, but not all, aspects of privacy as practiced in daily life. The definitions do not always reach the same conclusions as to the scope of privacy. Hence, deducing concrete legal rules from these theories is not an easy task. Furthermore, privacy is under attack by a number of different interest groups. Economists consider privacy an obstacle to the free flow of information.[49] Judge Richard Posner, for example, argues that much of the demand for privacy concerns discredible information, and the motive for concealment is often the desire to mislead others. False and incomplete representations lead to inefficient transactions and should therefore be limited.[50] Feminists criticize the distinction made between private and public privacy,[51] communitarians criticize

---

[45] See Alan F. Westin, PRIVACY AND FREEDOM (1971); Alan F. Westin, *Social and Political Dimensions of Privacy*, 59 J. OF SOCIAL ISSUES 431 (2003).

[46] Julie C. Inness, PRIVACY, INTIMACY, AND ISOLATION 7 (1992); Ellen Alderman & Caroline Kennedy, THE RIGHT TO PRIVACY 55–70 (New York, 1995).

[47] *See* Charles Fried, *Privacy [A Moral Analysis]*, in PHILOSOPHICAL DIMENSIONS OF PRIVACY 210 (1984).

[48] The idea of the panopticon was first made by Jeremy Bentham, who proposed an architectural model for a prison, in which inmates do not know if and when they are being watched by the guards. The idea was generalized by Michel Foucault, who argued that the panoptic gaze has a self-disciplinary power. See Michel Foucault, *Discipline and Punish*, in THE FOUCAULT READER 188 (Paul Rabinow ed., 1984). See also Oscar H. Gandi, THE PANOPTIC SORT: A POLITICAL ECONOMY OF PERSONAL INFORMATION (Boulder, 1993) and Jeffrey Rosen, THE UNWANTED GAZE: THE DESTRUCTION OF PRIVACY IN AMERICA (New York, 2001).

[49] See Richard Posner, *An Economic Analysis of Privacy*, in PHILOSOPHICAL DIMENSIONS OF PRIVACY: AN ANTHOLOGY 333–41 (Ferdinand David Schoeman ed., Cambridge, 1984).

[50] Richard A. Posner, *The Right to Privacy*, 12 GA. L. REV. 393 (1978). *See also* Paul M. Schwartz, *Privacy and Democracy in Cyberspace*, 52 VAND. L. REV. 1609, 1663 (1999) (referring to this problem as "data seclusion deception" but quickly dismissing it due to the "demands of the information age").

[51] For discussion of this critique and an attempt to reconcile it with privacy, see Judith Wagner DeCew, IN PURSUIT OF PRIVACY: LAW, ETHICS AND THE RISE OF TECHNOLOGY 81 (Cornell University Press, 1997).

the individualistic overtones of the right,[52] and those who wish to gather information and process it consider it an impingement on their freedom to conduct business.

One element in particular remains debated and controversial: Does (or should) the right to privacy cover an individual's control of information about him or her?[53] The question refers not only to sensitive information, but also to data that, at first glance, seems mundane, such as consumers' habits, surfing habits, and "technical" details. Those who respond in the affirmative argue that our privacy is gauged by our ability to determine when, how and to what extent information about us may be used.[54] Control of information about us is related to autonomy,[55] and more generally, to personal freedom and liberty.[56] When information about us is collected without our knowledge, consent or understanding, that is, when we are unaware of any privacy threat, we lose control over ourselves, our autonomy is compromised and our freedom to determine our own lives by ourselves is limited. When advertisers (re)create our consumerist profiles by reconstructing the bits and pieces of information that we constantly leave behind us, we ourselves become a commodity.

The right to privacy provides us with the ability to control the information and thus to define our own identity and prevent others from imposing their perceptions of who we are on us. The right to privacy allows us to resist becoming a commodity by designating the agencies with which we choose to have business or social contact and by limiting the proximity of commercial agencies in which we are not interested. In this context, the right to privacy allows us to determine our place in society.

Accordingly, the right to informational privacy is our right to control information concerning ourselves and the use of the information collected about us. We are entitled to determine the circumstances in which information about us will become public, that is, will be published, or will be accessible to the general public in another way.[57] This definition requires a decision as to what private information is entitled to protection and what rights of control we have in relation to this information. Thus,

---

[52] Amitai Etzioni, THE LIMITS OF PRIVACY 183–215 (New York, 1999).

[53] *E.g.*, Charles Fried considers that privacy is not only the other's absence of information about us, but also our ability to control information about us. See Fried, *supra* note 47; Charles Fried, *Privacy*, 77 YALE L.J. 475, 482 (1968).

[54] Westin, PRIVACY AND FREEDOM, *supra* note 45.

[55] *See* Julie E. Cohen, *Examined Lives: Informational Privacy and the Subject As Object*, 52 STAN. L. REV. 1373–438 (2000).

[56] *See* Fried, *supra* note 47.

[57] *See* Helen Nissenbaum, *Protecting Privacy in an Information Age: The Problem of Privacy in Public*, 17 L. & PHIL. 559 (1998).

in sociological terms, this definition of privacy marks the boundary line between the private and the public. However, this line is contested, and often blurred.

The controversy over information privacy, in other words, the scope of legal protection accorded to private data, is especially apparent in the opposite approaches taken by the United States and the European Union. While the latter acknowledges that the subject owns the data about him or her and should have control over it through data protection laws that heavily regulate the collection, processing and transfer of such data, the U.S. refuses to acknowledge a general right to data protection.[58] Instead, it has opted for a limited regulation, addressing only enumerated and a limited number of types of data. Prime examples include health data and financial data, but do not include data that at first glance seem mundane, such as surfing habits or consumer habits.[59]

Digital privacy. Given the philosophical debates concerning the basis for the right to privacy in general and the controversy over its scope and coverage of data protection (or information privacy) in particular, how does the right to privacy fare in the digital environment?[60] Even if we ignore traditional violations of privacy, such as the publication of personal information, the digital environment highlights the controversy over informational privacy.

Scott McNealy, the CEO of Sun Microsystems, famously stated, "you have zero privacy anyway, get over it."[61] As a descriptive statement, McNealy is closer to the truth than most people believe, although we do have some technical means to protect our privacy, generally known as Privacy Enhancing Technologies (PETs). However, the more interesting question is whether McNealy's statement is normatively desired. Perhaps privacy is dead?[62] Many like McNealy believe that it is indeed an obsolete idea that conflicts with and inhibits efficiency. Collecting data enables

---

[58] See Paul Schwartz & Joel R. Reidenberg, DATA PRIVACY LAW (Michie, 1996); Paul Schwartz & Joel R. Reidenberg, ONLINE SERVICES AND DATA PROTECTION LAW: REGULATORY RESPONSES (1998).

[59] *See* Daniel J. Solove, Marc Rotenberg & Paul M. Schwartz, INFORMATION PRIVACY LAW (2nd ed., Aspen, 2006).

[60] For recent discussions, see Daniel J. Solove, THE DIGITAL PERSON: TECHNOLOGY AND PRIVACY IN THE INFORMATION AGE (NYU Press, 2004).

[61] See Polly Sprenger, *Sun on Privacy: 'Get Over It'*, WIRED NEWS (January 26, 1999), available at http://www.wired.com/news/politics/0,1283,17538,00.html.

[62] See discussion in A. Michael Froomkin, *The Death of Privacy?*, 52 STAN. L. REV. 1461 (2000).

better customization and personalization of services (online as well as offline), and enables pinpoint targeting by advertisers.

Accordingly, and especially in the United States, we find a distinction based on the source of the threat to privacy. When the source is the State, privacy is considered to be a fundamental human right, protected by the Fourth Amendment to the Constitution as interpreted by the Supreme Court, but when the source of the threat to privacy stems from private entities, privacy issues are often ignored.[63]

The policy dilemma. The national security interests on which we focus here endanger privacy in the uncontroversial realm of the governmental paradigm, in which the government violates privacy. It should be clear at the outset that the government and its law enforcement agencies should be subject to constitutional scrutiny if and when they risk the privacy of citizens. Constitutional checks include, at the minimum, principles such as explicit authorization, proportionality and judicial oversight.

However, these minimal guarantees do not in themselves solve the dilemma. Indeed, security surveillance is required to prevent terror activities *ex ante*, and if prevention fails, then it might be needed to obtain evidence *ex post*. Given the civilian nature of the Internet and the terrorist activity within, and given that the identity of the terrorist is often unknown in advance, gathering intelligence inevitably affects the privacy of innocent citizens. Information about their perfectly legal activities might be collected, analyzed, and exposed, in the course of determining whether there is a terrorist hiding among us. In this sense, we need to appreciate the grave difficulty and hence the challenge that the intelligence agencies face. In late 2006, Israel's General Security Service (Shin Bet) launched an unprecedented open campaign to recruit computer programmers. The Head of the Shin Bet, Yuval Diskin explained in an unusual online video that, "we are looking for a needle in a stack of needles, and that's even harder than finding a needle in a haystack."[64]

---

[63] This view directly conflicts with the European view, a conflict that complicates trans-Atlantic data transactions. To overcome this problem, the U.S. and the EU negotiated the Safe Harbor Agreement. For a discussion, see Jan Dhont, Maria Veronica Perez Asinari, Yves Poullet, with Joel R. Reidenberg and Lee Bygrave, Safe Harbor Decision Implementation Study (European Commission, 2004), available at http://ec.europa.eu/justice_home/fsj/privacy/docs/studies/safe-harbour-2004_en.pdf.

[64] See http://www.shabak.gov.il/it (last visited Oct. 2006). See also Associated Press, *Shin Bet Launches Recruitment Drive*, Jerusalem Post (September 5, 2006), available at http://www.jpost.com /servlet/Satellite?pagename=JPost%2FJPArticle%2FShowFull&cid=1154526009320.

Thus, balancing privacy and security interests is inevitable. Legally, the balance might be conducted explicitly, as in Israeli constitutional law, or implicitly, in interpreting various terms and concepts within existing law. Details also matter. Technological options should be evaluated to assess which one may be the least invasive of privacy. For example, one could consider a method that enables the State to intercept all information without filtering and to analyze only the suspicious information using data mining technologies. This possibility allows access, after the communication took place, to information that initially did not seem dangerous.[65] The events of September 11, 2001 illustrate this point. The terrorists who planned the attacks communicated with each other via email. They did not arouse suspicion in real time. However, after the events, this information was extremely relevant in locating those responsible for the attack. Nonetheless, interception of all the information traveling through the Internet can have many indirect effects on the rights of innocent users. Individuals who wish to transmit personal information unrelated to terror or harmful acts may fear to do so, knowing that this information may be intercepted and documented by the State and even be used against them in due course.

A second method would be to allow the State to eavesdrop on all information and to intercept only that which it suspects might be harmful to the public order. In this scenario, the data is not recorded, guaranteeing that it will not be possible in the future to reconstruct information that was monitored. This option is less harmful than the previous one, but there are other crucial issues that arise from this option, such as determining the degree of suspicion that allows interception.

1.3.2 Freedom of Expression

Security needs also clash with the fundamental right to freedom of expression. Free speech jurisprudence (in the American jargon) or freedom of expression (the European term) in its absolute sense is the freedom to express opinions in any way without any fear of prejudice to any interest of the speaker. In this context, prior restraint is the strongest case of censorship, but modern jurisprudence includes many other, less overt governmental actions as forms of censorship, such as taxes imposed on

---

[65] For a detailed technological proposal along these lines, see Bracha Shapira, *A Content-Based Model for Web-monitoring*, in FIGHTING TERROR IN CYBERSPACE 63.

newspapers only, or vague, overly broad legislative definitions. The latter are problematic because they have a chilling effect on people's actions leading to an individual's curbing his speech for fear of straying into illegal areas. For example, a legal rule that criminalizes the online transfer of pornographic material without defining the term "pornographic material" would be vague and probably overly broad. This vagueness might cause a law-abiding citizen to refrain from a perfectly legal action, such as emailing a friend an artistic photograph of a nude person. The law frowns upon the causes of such chilling effects, and tends to invalidate them.

The information age in general and the Internet in particular have raised many questions concerning freedom of expression. The Internet constitutes "a free market of ideas," providing a platform for expression and allowing users to share their opinions without any geographic restrictions. The capacity to transmit messages to millions by the click of a mouse and at low cost makes the Internet the most democratic communication means created to date. Indeed, in the 1990s, once the free speech capacity of the Internet became apparent, many celebrated this form of "cheap speech"[66]. For a while, it seemed online, "everyone can be a speaker." The difficulty of enforcing local censorship and the demise of traditional intermediaries such as publishers or music labels were celebrated.

However, as the Internet matured a bit, the rosy picture became murkier. Some countries impose restrictions on the use of Internet by their citizens, and limit access quite effectively to content of which the government disapproves.[67] The digital divide leaves many outside the marketplace of ideas.[68] There is a concern that the vast quantity of speech will result in a fragmentation of the public sphere, to the extent that there is not one marketplace of ideas, but many that do not communicate with one another.[69] Others point to the overload of information, which renders the process of rational decision-making (individual or collective) almost impossible.[70] Instead of the old intermediaries, we have come to realize that there are new, no less and sometime even more, powerful

---

[66] *See e.g.*, Eugene Volokh, *Cheap Speech and What it Will Do*, 104 YALE L. J. 1805 (1995).

[67] See the annual reports of Freedom House on the status of free speech around the world, available at http://www.freedomhouse.org.

[68] See the series of reports by the U.S. Department of Commerce, National Telecommunications and Information Administration (NTIA), *Falling through the Net*, published in 1995, 1998, 1999, 2000, available at http://www.ntia.doc.gov.

[69] *See* Cass Sunstein, REPUBLIC.COM (Princeton University Press, 2002).

[70] *See* Shenk, *supra* note 35.

intermediaries,[71] namely ISPs and other gatekeepers such as search engines.[72] These relatively recent realizations do not mean that freedom of speech does not exist on the Internet; it does, and indeed, the Internet's attributes are a cause for celebration. However, we do need to be aware of these drawbacks in order to address them.

Free speech is now under further pressure, this time from the need for security. Free speech is threatened directly by terror propaganda, and indirectly by the monitoring of Internet traffic and communications.

Surveillance causes a chilling effect. The right to privacy is necessary in order to exercise freedom of expression. When a person knows that she is under surveillance or that her words and deeds are being recorded, she is liable to avoid speaking freely. Sometimes knowledge of the use of surveillance techniques, even if they are not actually in constant use, is sufficient to lead to self-censorship. A user might refrain from writing, publishing, or communicating his or her genuine thoughts for fear that they might be misunderstood, mislabeled as terror propaganda, or caught in the net of the law enforcement agencies monitoring the Internet.[73] Furthermore, anonymity is often understood as a derivative of privacy, but it also underpins free speech. American courts protect anonymity because of its relationship to free speech.[74]

As for terror propaganda, it is first necessary to clarify the protected interest within freedom of expression. The concern is not the fate of the terrorist's right to free speech, as the terrorist is usually beyond the reach of local authorities and in many cases, the speech is (constitutionally) considered illegal. The concern lies with the impact on the public's right to know, that is, the public's right to access information and make judgments itself. Indeed, it is not always clear what the benefit of disclosing the terrorist's speech might be. In many cases, it is probably of no benefit whatsoever to the public. However, the principle of free speech assumes that exposure to another opinion, even a roguish opinion, has advantages. It strengthens the counter-expression, challenges the "truth," exposes the true face of the adversary, and obliges us to reexamine our own positions.

---

[71] See Andrew L. Shapiro, THE CONTROL REVOLUTION: HOW THE INTERNET IS PUTTING INDIVIDUALS IN CHARGE AND CHANGING THE WORLD (Century Foundation, 1999).

[72] See Niva Elkin-Koren, *Let the Crawlers Crawl: On Virtual Gatekeepers and the Right to Exclude Indexing*, 26 DAYTON L. REV. 180 (2001).

[73] *See* Flaherty, *supra* note 39, at 831, 843.

[74] See, for example, the discussion about ordering ISPs to reveal the identity of anonymous users, John Doe v. Patrick Cahill (Supreme Court of Delaware, Oct. 5, 2005).

This is the classic explanation provided by John Stewart Mill for the protection of freedom of speech.[75]

According to Harvard Law Professor Alan Dershowitz, freedom of speech is so important that it is worth living with some of its abuse for the greater importance of the principle. Yet, he would also agree that there are limits that must be set. In any case, the accepted justifications of freedom of speech assume that it is not the State's role to interfere and to restrict access to speech.

However, protecting free speech in an absolute way would mean that no steps could be taken against terror propaganda and no surveillance would be permitted. Hence, we are left with the difficult task of balancing free speech concerns with security needs. The idea of balancing in constitutional law is a foreign concept in U.S. law,[76] which applies a different constitutional methodology for addressing such questions, namely, categorization. Some categories of speech are not covered by the First Amendment.[77] Obscenity is a well-known example, as is the category of "fighting words," defined by the Supreme Court as "those [words] which by their very utterance inflict injury or tend to incite an immediate breach of the peace."[78] Later on, the Court narrowed down this category.[79] Privacy issues are usually addressed in a separate legal category, under the Fourth Amendment to the U.S. Constitution, which allows greater interpretive leeway.

Other legal systems, such as European Law and Israeli law, do not shy away from explicit balancing. Article 10(2) of the European Convention on Human Rights states:

> The exercise of these freedoms, since it carries with it duties and responsibilities, may be subject to such formalities, conditions, restrictions or penalties as are prescribed by law and are necessary in a democratic society, in the interests of national security, territorial integrity or public safety, for the prevention of disorder or crime, for the protection of health or morals, for the protection of the reputation or rights of others, for preventing the disclosure of information

---

[75] *See* John Stuart Mill, ON LIBERTY 5–9 (Wordsworth Classics ed., 1996) (Roberts & Green, London: Longman 1869).

[76] See T.A. Alienkoff, *Constitutional Law in the Age of Balancing*, 96 YALE L. J. 943 (1986).

[77] The categories were listed in a Supreme Court case, Chaplinsky v. New Hampshire, 315 U.S. 568 (1942). For discussion of the term "coverage," see Frederick Schauer, *Free Speech: A Philosophical Enquiry* (Cambridge, UK, 1982).

[78] *Chaplinsky, supra* note 77.

[79] *See* R.A.V. v. City of St. Paul, 505 U.S. 377 (1992),

received in confidence, or for maintaining the authority and impartiality of the judiciary.[80]

This formulation allows for a balance between freedom of expression and national security interests, if some conditions are met: the restriction of free speech should be prescribed by law, it should be necessary, and the European Courts added another criterion, that of proportionality. The restriction on freedom of expression should be proportionate to the legitimate aim pursued.[81]

Does this balance apply in the digital environment? One position argues that the constitutional balance between free speech and national security needs is a moral judgment and is not, and should not be, technology-dependent. Therefore, the arrival of the new medium does not modify the fundamental principles.[82] The opposite position maintains that the existing rules should not be applied to the digital medium and that the new medium calls for a reexamination of the existing checks and balances. According to this approach, legal interference in freedom of expression should be reduced (even to the point of disappearing) in the traditional media as well. A third, middle position argues that the new technology calls for a legal modification, but one that does not have to be dramatically different from rules that are currently in place. The legal rules should be formulated according to the same principles and values that have been used to date, but should be adapted to the new medium according to its unique characteristics. Regulation of expression on the Internet involves new considerations because of its democratic possibilities. The ease of accessibility, reduced cost of expression, and the possibility of interactive dialogue make the user not only a passive consumer, but also enable the user to choose to become an active participant.[83] Accordingly, regulation, even if its aim is legitimate, may have a negative effect on all of these factors. Existing law appears to tend toward this golden mean. The starting point in formulating the legal rules is the existing moral balances, but their

---

[80] . ECHR, Art. 10(2) (emphasis added).

[81] *See e.g.*, Bowman v. United Kingdom, 26 Eur. H.R. Rep. 1, 13 (1998). See the discussion in Michael Supperstone & Jason Coppel, *Judicial Review After the Human Rights Act*, 1999 Eur. Hum. Rts. L. Rev. 301, 312–13; Takis Tridimas, The General Principles of EC Law 89–94 (1999).

[82] Not surprisingly, courts hold the position that the pre-digital law applies to the new media, with necessary but technical changes. See, for example, the various opinions in Ashcroft v. American Civil Liberties Union, 535 U.S. 564 (2002).

[83] For a comparison between the characteristics of the existing technologies and the characteristics of the Internet, see Reno v. ACLU, 521 U.S. 844 (1997).

application to the Internet must take into account its special characteristics.[84] Later on, we will return to the legal analysis.

1.3.3 Enforcement

The threats of global terrorism require governments to undertake enforcement measures in the online environment. However, the traditional enforcement mechanisms of states are fundamentally challenged by the online environment. Conventional enforcement tools may not fit the new digital arena, especially against individual users who might engage in hostile hacking, the distribution of terrorist propaganda, or fundraising to support illegal terrorist organizations. The most obvious reason is that states may exercise power within their jurisdiction, while hostile activities may originate outside their territorial borders. Furthermore, the online environment makes it easy to disguise the physical identity of offenders. Virtual identities may not be easy to monitor and sanction because they can be multiplied and are fleeting in nature. Some users may use different addresses for different purposes. Others may avoid responsibility for online harm by changing their IP address, thus escaping any sanctions against them, such as restricting their access to an online area. To make users accountable for their online behavior, it is necessary to match users' online identities represented by IP addresses or domain names with their physical identity. Such a match between online identities and identifiable individuals can be made by online service providers. However, such a central identification system may threaten users' privacy and allow Internet Service Providers (ISPs) a high degree of control over online activities. This potential control may threaten the civil liberties of users.

When online hostile activity, such as the distribution of terrorist propaganda, is hosted by online service providers, governments may try to prevent this activity by approaching online service providers (such as website storage service providers, managers of sites, and those who host online forums). Clearly, there is a practical difficulty in restricting the speech

---

[84] Retired Israeli Justice Mishael Cheshin, in his capacity as Chairman of the Israeli Central Elections Committee, ruled that the restrictions in the Elections Act (Campaign Broadcasting) should not be extended to the speech of a politician in an Internet chat room. See Court Action 16/2001 Shas – World Union of Torah Observant Sephardim v. M.K. Ophir Pines, Deputy Chairman of the Central Elections Committee (decision of the Chairman of the Central Elections Committee (January 30, 2001)). Among other considerations, his reasoning was based on the special characteristics of the Internet and on the importance of freedom of expression.

of terrorist organizations, because they are not within the country's borders and, in any case (even if they do work within its borders), they do not obey the law. Therefore, quite naturally, attention has turned to the various intermediaries that allow the terrorist organizations, by their very activities, to disseminate their messages on their sites. These intermediaries include Internet providers that store terrorist sites on their servers, providers that allow subscribers access to such sites (whether they are stored on their servers or not), Internet sites that create links to terrorist sites, sites that operate interactive services (such as forums and chat rooms), or search engines that facilitate access to illegal materials. These mediators constitute a kind of technical bottleneck; they are a convenient point at which it is possible to curtail the scope of the terrorist organizations' propaganda activity. This possibility leads to the question of the liability of online intermediaries for injurious behavior inflicted by their subscribers. Is it legally possible and morally necessary to make service providers liable for the expression of speech they make possible through their services? It is worthwhile to explore this issue of indirect liability and examine the implications of creating legislation that addresses the liability of service providers.

The issue of the liability of online service providers is not exclusive to terrorist "speech." It also arises in the context of other harmful expressions, such as defamation, copyright infringement, dissemination of pornography, and violation of privacy. Policy making in this area should strike a balance between enforcement efficiency and the desire to prevent and curtail harmful expression and the value of the Internet as an open forum for public dialogue and economic growth. In the following section, we will review the considerations that arise in placing liability on Internet providers and discuss the advantages and implications of such a rule. We then present the legal models developed in this context.

Considerations in placing liability on online intermediaries. Enforcement by intermediaries is attractive because the global nature of the Internet challenges existing law enforcement authorities and legal institutions. The online environment makes it increasingly difficult to locate the original speaker and to enforce local laws against terrorist propaganda disseminated on the Internet, which is a global network. The cross-border nature of the Internet weakens the effectiveness of regulation by making it more difficult to identify injurers and bring them to justice.[85] The global nature of the Internet further weakens the legitimacy of regulation that would be

---

[85] See David R. Johnson & David G. Post, *The New 'Civic Virtue' of the Internet*, 1998 ANN. REV. INST. FOR INFO. STUD. 23.

justifiable within territorial borders.[86] Given that terrorist activities take place across national borders, regulating such activity by one country may affect citizens of another country.[87]

The difficulty in identifying and locating the speaker and enforcing the law in relation to terrorist organizations makes online intermediaries an attractive target for enforcement efforts. Placing liability on the providers has several advantages in this context.

First, it is easier to locate the service provider than the individual end user who disseminated the terrorist propaganda.[88] The provider conducts business openly and, over time, has a physical and business presence and financial and legal activity that can be easily located. Placing liability on intermediaries eases enforcement and facilitates prevention. Intermediaries could block illegal content or disconnect the service that facilitates illegal activities. Furthermore, when intermediaries are at risk of being held liable for terrorist propaganda, they are likely to take steps to minimize their legal exposure. Liability would create incentives for the service provider to screen site contents before their publication in order to prevent dissemination of contents that may entail a legal liability.

However, it is not always obvious that what one country sees as "propaganda terror" will be regarded as such by another country. An example of this problem can be seen in the LICRA v. Yahoo! case. In this case, the French court ruled that the American company Yahoo! must comply with French law forbidding dissemination of Nazi articles on the Internet. The court ruled that Yahoo! must block the access of users in France to sites in which such articles are offered for sale.[89] However, an American court ruled that Yahoo! did not have to comply with the French order.[90] Since most anti-regime organizations generally work outside the country they target, the solution to this problem lies in creating international regulation treaties.

---

[86] For the perception of the Internet as a global enterprise that lies beyond the reach of laws of any particular government, see *id.* at 26–31. For criticism of that viewpoint, see Neil Weinstock Netanel, *Cyberspace Self-Governance: A Skeptical View from Liberal Democratic Theory*, 88 CAL. L. REV. 395 (2000).

[87] David R. Johnson & David G. Post, *Law and Borders: The Rise of Law in Cyberspace*, 48 STAN. L. REV. 1367 (1996); Joel Reidenberg, *Yahoo and Democracy on the Internet*, 42 JURIMETRICS 261 (2002).

[88] Tsfati & Weimann, *supra* note 26, at 58.

[89] See League Against Racism and Antisemitism (LICRA v. Yahoo! Inc., Yahoo! France) County Court, Paris, November 20, 2000.

[90] See Yahoo!, Inc., v. La Ligue Contre le Racisme et L'antisemitisme, 169 F.Supp.2d 1181 (Northern District Court of California, 2001).

Alongside the advantages of placing liability for harmful content on the service provider, there may be undesirable consequences. Placing responsibility on service providers will oblige them to take measures to avoid liability, such as the creation of a control and surveillance mechanism. The service provider may also require legal advice or insurance. These resources have a high financial cost.

Usually, it can be assumed that the provider will pass the cost on to its consumer public, dispersing the damage through subscriber fees. Thus, the imposition of additional costs on the service provider actually means that the provider's subscribers, namely, the users, not the general tax-paying public, will bear the cost of the fight against terror. A further possible consequence might be the raising of prices for Internet services, the result of which would be a burden on the other operations taking place online, such as research, development, education, and commerce.

Furthermore, the negative legal and economic consequences create an incentive among service providers not to provide interactive services when the operation of such services involves a risk. On the one hand, the provider is not the source of the content and therefore does not control the content disseminated by the users. On the other hand, these services constitute the source of the Internet's force and contain economic and democratic possibilities.

Placing liability on service providers has an immediate implication for freedom of expression. Due to fear of liability, the provider may prefer to curb a potentially problematic user's advertising or activity and will therefore tend to engage in private censorship. In this way, the vital oxygen of freedom of expression will be limited. In situations of preventing terror, the main objective is to prevent the damage in advance, not to pay compensation afterwards.

In fact, self-censorship of this sort constitutes privatization of the enforcement system. The service provider's considerations in the control and surveillance that it operates will be economic cost-benefit considerations. Clearly, these are legitimate considerations from the provider's viewpoint. However, these considerations will actually replace the complex checks and balances developed in case law – checks and balances designed to protect human rights, on the one hand, and to guarantee the public interest, on the other. Moreover, the provider's discretion is not subject to the rules of procedural and constitutional law, as the provider is not elected and is not accountable to the public.

Models for liability of intermediaries. Existing models of legislation can be classified into three main types of regulation: regulation of liability at one end, regulation of immunity at the other end and regulation of conditional and restricted immunity in the middle. In Europe, a uniform regulation applies to all types of infringements and damages, whereas in the United States, there are several legal regimes that apply to different types of damage: defamation, copyright infringement, or others.[91] It should be pointed out that these models developed within the framework of civil law as the result of situations in which individuals were injured. Consequently, any analogy to criminal law and national security should be drawn with caution. The standard of liability in the criminal context is higher and requires proof of criminal intent beyond probable doubt.

One possible model holds intermediaries strictly liable for the various activities carried out through their facilities. This model exists, for instance, in the civil legislation that places liability not only on the direct injurer or infringer, but also on others who contributed indirectly or otherwise assisted the injurer. For instance, under U.S. law, publishers of traditional media (books, newspapers) would be held strictly liable for all content they published, even if authored by someone else. Similarly, in the Israeli Defamation Law 1965, liability is placed not only on the defamer but also on the "editor of the media," "responsible party of the media," "printer and distributor."

At the other end of the spectrum, full immunity is provided to online intermediaries. This approach was adopted by the U.S. Congress in § 230 of the Telecommunications Act of 1996.[92] Section 230 exempted interactive computer service providers from strict liability for publishing injurious content that originated with their subscribers[93]:

> No provider or user of an interactive computer service shall be treated as the publisher or speaker of any information provided by another information content provider.[94]

---

[91] For a comparative discussion, see Kamiel Koelman & Bernt Hugenholtz, *Online Service Provider Liability for Copyright Infringement*, WIPO Workshop on Service Provider Liability (Geneva, 1999).

[92] Pub. L. No. 104–104, 110 Stat. 56 (1996) (codified as amended in scattered sections of 47 U.S.C.).

[93] 47 U.S.C. § 230 (2000); see also Zeran v. America Online, Inc., 129 F.3d 327, 330 (4th Cir. 1997) (holding that "[b]y its plain language, § 230 creates a federal immunity to any cause of action that would make service providers liable for information originating with a third-party user of the service. Specifically, § 230 precludes courts from entering claims that would place a computer service provider in a publisher's role."); Blumenthal v. Drudge, 992 F. Supp. 44 (D.D.C. 1998); Jane Doe v. America Online, Inc., 783 So.2d 1010 (Fla. 2001).

[94] See 47 U.S.C. § 230(c)(1)

U.S law distinguishes between the publisher, who has absolute liability, and the distributor, who is liable if he knew or should have known of the damage or infringement caused by third parties. According to its wording, § 230 grants immunity only from absolute liability. However, this section has been interpreted at length by the courts in the United States, which determined that the service providers are immune in any case, even if they were given notice of the damage/infringement.[95]

An example of such a situation is the case of Zeran vs. America Online (AOL), a leading American ISP. In that case, information was disseminated on an AOL site about an individual, stating that he supported the blowing up of the Federal building in Oklahoma and was selling T-shirts with an inscription expressing his support. The person in question informed AOL that this was a lie, but AOL did not remove the advertisement from the Internet – an omission that led to his action against AOL. The court ruled that Congress's goal was to provide broad protection to the ISPs. Therefore, the term "publisher" used in 47 U.S.C. § 230(c) must be interpreted in a broad sense and for this case must also include the meaning of distributor. The court assumed that, unless exempted, ISPs would be forced to decide whether to publish, edit, or withdraw a posting every time a notice is served by a party claiming injury.[96] This costly decision-making process would induce ISPs to remove every controversial message upon notice, and would therefore lead to the chilling effect the law sought to avoid.[97]

In other words, the liability of a publisher or a distributor would not apply to the ISP. In effect, the law gave Internet Service Providers immunity from damage claims by anyone injured because of defamation. Likewise, immunity was also granted to the provider, vis-à-vis the publisher, for acts of self-censorship that the service provider carried out.

While perfect immunity creates no incentives to intervene in injurious content originated by subscribers, immunity that is contingent upon undertaking enforcement measures may lead to over-enforcement. Therefore, a third model, which lies in between the two extremes, would make

---

[95] See *Zeran* at 327. For criticism of this ruling, see the minority opinion in Doe v. American Online, Inc., 783 So.2d 1010 (S.Ct. Fla. 2001).

[96] The amount of information communicated via interactive computer services is therefore staggering. The specter of tort liability in an area of such prolific speech would have an obvious chilling effect. It would be impossible for service providers to screen each of their millions of postings for possible problems. Faced with potential liability for each message republished by their services, interactive computer service providers might choose to severely restrict the number and type of messages posted.-*Zeran*, 129 F.3d at 331.

[97] *Id.* at 333.

liability conditional. According to this model, the provider would be exempted from liability for injuries caused by its subscribers, as long as the provider meets certain requirements established by the law. For instance, § 512 of the US Copyright Act, as amended by the DMCA (hereinafter: "safe harbor provisions"), immunizes ISPs from liability for monetary damages and limits the availability of injunctive relief, with certain limitations and in exchange for help with copyright enforcement. The DMCA safe harbor provisions establish a detailed exemption for certain online intermediaries who meet three types of conditions.[98] The first condition relates to the nature of the provider, namely, that it is an online service provider as defined by law.[99]

The second condition relates to the type of activities. Immunity will apply only to "transitory digital network communications,"[100] temporary storage during transmission (use of caching),[101] storage,[102] and "information location tools."[103] The third condition requires that an ISP adopt and implement policies that facilitate the enforcement of copyright on its system. The safe harbor regime introduced several mechanisms for enforcing copyright. First, there is the notice and take-down procedure, which requires ISPs to remove infringing materials residing on their systems upon notice from the copyright owner, or to block access to sites where the infringing material resides on an online location outside the United States.[104] The notice and take-down procedure strictly defines the notice requirements and the procedures to be followed upon notice, thus providing ISPs with guidelines regarding the management of infringement claims. A second enforcement mechanism requires ISPs to terminate the accounts of repeat offenders.[105] Third, § 512(h) requires disclosure of the identities of offenders upon subpoena,[106] but ISPs are not required to identify those offenders absent a subpoena.[107] Finally, ISPs are required not to interfere with standard technical measures employed by copyright holders.[108]

---

[98] 17 U.S.C. § 512.
[99] *Id.* § 512(k).
[100] *Id.* § 512(a).
[101] *Id.* § 512(b).
[102] *Id.* § 512(c).
[103] *Id.* § 512(d).
[104] *Id.* § 512(j)(1)(B).
[105] *Id.* § 512(i)(1).
[106] *Id.* § 512(h).
[107] *Id.* § 512(i)(1)(B).
[108] *Id.*

The rule adopted in the European Directive regarding e-commerce also establishes an exemption from liability for certain actions when the conditions listed are fulfilled.[109]

1.4 Electronic Commerce and Innovation

This subsection addresses several strategies aimed at strengthening government control over the distribution and use of encryption. As Niva Elkin-Koren noted, "From the standpoint of purely security concerns, counter-terrorist efforts could benefit if encryption were used exclusively by states, and terrorists had no access to it. Such exclusivity is not feasible, however, and any attempt to enhance the control of government over the use and development of encryption means also comes at a price. Strategies may take the form of restrictions on the export of certain encryption technologies, prohibitions regarding the use of encryption technology by anyone other than the authorities, or, the most extreme form – restrictions on the development of certain technologies. Another strategy would require developers to design their products so as to allow the State 'back door' access. Such policies could affect the behavior of scientists in the encryption research community and investments by the private sector in R&D. When governments are considering monitoring and restricting encryption, they must consider the consequences of any such regulation for research and development in cryptology and for emerging markets."

1.4.1 Ramifications for Research and Development

In the area of computers in general, constant development has far-reaching economic significance. High technology companies must constantly innovate and update their products in order to remain competitive. The average time between the release of one product and the next is at most 18 months. This timeline is particularly true for methods of encryption and protection for systems, as there is a constant, parallel effort to develop the means to break through them.

---

[109] See § § 12–15 of Directive 2000/31/EC of the European Parliament and of the Council of June 8, 2000 on certain legal aspects of information society services, in particular electronic commerce, in the internal market ('Directive on electronic commerce') OJL 178.

Again Elkin-Koren points out, "Encryption is not the sole domain of governments. Encryption technologies are developed by the private sector for commercial purposes such as data protection, privacy, secrecy, and the protection of intellectual property. Those keys are based on the same encryption technology often used by government. The difference between encryption technologies is often their extensiveness, which depends on the sensitivity of the information they are tailored to secure."

Those involved in the private sector have a clear interest in developing their products in line with the demands of the market, without any restrictions. Consequently, policy makers must consider the potential consequences of encryption policy on research and development by the private sector: What economic influence would regulation have on incentives for private companies? Would such consequences be desirable for private companies and for the market as a whole?

Governmental non-intervention is the desired approach from the point of view of industry concerning regulating encryption and export of the means of encryption. During the period when restrictions were more stringent, computer companies protested against them and called for reform. Their call was supported by the fact that these restrictions had a serious economic effect on American companies. The CSPP (Computer Systems Policy Project) called for a change in policy and an opening of borders, because export restrictions were affecting the ability of American companies to compete effectively in world markets.

Koops[110] considered the possibility of a prohibition on encryption. In his view, when a problem arises in society as the result of a particular element, the natural tendency of the State is to make that element illegal. This approach is logical when dealing with an element or activity whose results or influences are all negative. However, this logic does not apply so clearly to encryption, which has many positive aspects. Koops contends that making encryption illegal is not a realistic option, even though the possibility of prohibiting encryption has been raised by a number of governments around the world.

The prohibition of encryption could be absolute or partial. A partial prohibition of encryption would result in licensing only weaker encryption programs and in selectivity with respect to which bodies would be eligible for licensing. The problem with prohibiting encryption is that it would be impossible to enforce. Furthermore, decryption efforts aimed at

---

[110] Bert-Jaap Koops, THE CRYPTO CONTROVERSY: A KEY CONFLICT IN THE INFORMATION SOCIETY 125–31 (The Hague, Kluwer Law International, 1999).

new encryption technologies are more diffused and difficult to monitor. Challenging initiatives to current encryption will continue to evolve, even if only by non-law-abiding parties. In the end, law-abiding citizens' rights would be infringed upon, while terrorists would be unaffected and would continue in their illegal activities.

Undoubtedly, prohibiting encryption would have negative consequences on the individual and on the collective as a whole. Restrictions on encryption technologies may deny individuals access to products that could be used to secure their privacy and intellectual property, thus undermining the delicate balance between the liberty of citizens and the power of governments. At the collective level, encryption prohibitions could be harmful to the economy. International trade would be affected, as companies would not be able to communicate securely with each other. If encryption prohibitions were put in place only on a national level and not enforced globally, then companies in countries imposing such prohibitions would not be able to compete with their counterparts from other countries, thus damaging the economies of those countries restricting encryption. If a better protocol were developed in another country that could replace old standards, it would put local companies at a serious disadvantage.

These scenarios suggest that the regulation of encryption, in whatever form, is not economically efficient. Economic theory makes it clear that the market operates best when it is free, without any intervention. The picture changes, of course, when there are market failures. Then there is a need for governmental intervention. From a purely economic standpoint, the question is whether terrorist activities concealed by encryption, and the breaking of encryption by hostile elements, constitute market failures that would justify regulatory intervention. It seems that the best way of dealing with the problem is to allow industry to continue developing protections against such threats under competitive market conditions.

1.4.2 Encryption Regulation and Electronic Commerce

Encryption and encryption systems constitute a system of "locks and keys" in the digital environment that protect increasing amounts of personal information, email communications, electronic commerce, and other data that could be used to infer information that is considered private. Encryption keys are essential for electronic commerce and are made widely available in electronic products by commercial entities.

Encryption could ensure the secrecy of online payments, the privacy of email exchanges, or the protection of copyrighted music against unauthorized use. Consequently, the regulation of encryption might affect not only the cryptologists and businesses that would like to implement it in their products, but also the population as a whole. If encryption were not available, individual users would be exposed to fraud and abuse and would be vulnerable to both commercial entities and government agents.

Encryption does not differentiate between classes of users or methods of use, and the same level or strength of encryption applies, for good or for bad, to both the innocent user and the criminal or terrorist. If we stretch the locks/keys metaphor, we can understand that individuals have the right to privacy and to install "locks" on the "doors" that access their private information. However, there are restrictions on the types of "locks" one can use; not everyone can build the fence or install the lock he wants. There are always controls that restrict him – starting with the production of protective devices, their installation, and quality control – all the way to marketing.

The reasons for these controls are many and vary from one field to another. In abstract terms, regulation needs to take into account the extreme cases in society, not the innocent citizen. For our discussion, the extreme case is the terrorist who, in the technological age, uses electronic communications and other methods protected by encryption in exactly the same way as "old style" terrorists used physical items protected or concealed by physical means. For both "old style" devices and modern means, there are and need to be ways of breaking into them, a kind of "back door" key held by governmental authorities.

What makes encryption methods unique, however, is that they are designed from the beginning to conceal; it is insufficient to grant specific authorization to break a certain encryption (as is done in the case of wiretapping, for example). It has to be ensured ahead of time that the technological possibility of breaking the encryption exists. If governments want to ensure that they can decrypt every encrypted communication, they may try to impose certain technological requirements on device manufactures or providers of infrastructure. The most detailed example of a technological capability requirement is the Communications Assistance for Law Enforcement Act of 1994 (CALEA). CALEA mandates that telecommunications services design their technology so it can be wiretapped by the government pursuant to a lawful authorization or a court order. CALEA does not require a specific technological design or prohibit any particular technology, but does require that the design enables the government to access call-identifying information and allows for the transmission of the intercepted information to the government. Similarly, if a *key escrow* is required, producers who use encryption would deposit the keys needed for decryption with a third party, so that once the government is authorized to decrypt content, it could obtain the keys for that purpose.

Key escrow was very controversial. A long-running debate on this issue took place in the United States about the extent to which the Administration should be permitted to maintain the option of using "back door" access, that is, a kind of "master key" or algorithm that would allow the re-creation of private keys. The use of such keys obviously would be subject to various limitations, such as court approval and division of the implementing body into two, which would then hold the key jointly.

As the level of supervision and control over local production and importation of encryption products increases, so does the possibility that the State will access encrypted material via these back doors – resulting in a likely violation of citizens' privacy. Giving the State back door control over encryption mechanisms can result in both direct harm and indirect damage.

Providing the technical and legal possibility of intercepting and deciphering encrypted materials may harm even law-abiding citizens who are not under suspicion. Such harm could occur, for example, when the circumstances require examination of material or correspondence passing through an Internet server that serves thousands of innocent civilians, but also a suspected terrorist. This harm is in addition to the inherent violation of rights involved in police investigations of those who are innocent, because they have not yet been proven guilty. Furthermore, there is always the possibility of error and false accusations.

The fact that the government has control over the means of encryption or the possibility of decryption, and the existence of back door access, even if never used, creates certain apprehension among the public. This apprehension may serve as a chilling factor that deters people from using digital databases, online services, or electronic commerce, with negative repercussions for the economy. Schilling has argued,[111] based on game theory, that when regulation is increased, the level of Internet use by private users will decrease. This decline in use will occur in spite of the public's interest in regulation as a means to prevent crime and fight terrorism. A high level of regulation would limit the options for encryption that become available on the market. Without strong encryption to protect their

---

[111] Thorsten Schilling, *Raiding the Net: Is There a Need for an Information Highway Patrol?* 1 Netnomics 37, 51 (1999).

privacy, individuals may not feel sufficiently secure to use the Internet for commerce. A similar argument was raised in a paper submitted to the American government by EPIC (Electronic Privacy Information Council) on the public's interests regarding the regulation of electronic trade.[112] EPIC concludes that the Administration should avoid regulatory intervention in the area of encryption and let the market develop strong encryption tools in order to encourage use of the Internet in general, and participation in e-commerce in particular. If the State were to impose broad restrictions on encryption, the developing area of e-commerce, which is an effective and desirable economic tool, would be directly harmed and would lose its effectiveness.

---

[112] See Public Comment on Barriers to Electronic Commerce- Comment on Behalf of Electronic Privacy Information Center (EPIC) by Sarah Andrews, Policy Analyst, and Andrew Shen, Policy Analyst. (March 17, 2000), available at http://osecnt13.osec.doc.gov/ecommerce/barriers.nsf /review/46112999BDD282C9852568A6000093AF

Chapter 2
The Legal Situation: Prevention
and Enforcement in the Information Age

In this chapter, we will examine the development of the legal frame-work internationally, in the United States, in the European Union, and in selected other countries in relation to the issues outlined in Chapter 1. An examination of some of the laws that have evolved in these countries will offer insight into the delicate balance that modern nations strive for between the need for security and the preservation of civil rights. The law is changing rapidly in this regard, with updates that might suggest an on-line book and not a printed one. What is current today, may be history tomorrow.

Nevertheless, the principles and processes for addressing these funda-mental issues are rooted in what we present here. The terrorist is ever more sophisticated, and so too must be the law. Grappling with the difficult balancing act between security needs, the legal rights of the individual and the ever evolving developments of technology is a daunting challenge for mankind.

The means of prevention and enforcement operated by government authorities are guided, at least on the face of it, by regulations and prin-ciples of public law, three of which are discussed below. First, state authorities are subject to constitutional law and basic rights of the nor-mative framework, wherein all activities should be balanced with respect to human rights.

Second, the authorities are subject to the principles of administrative law, which delineate a framework of action in pursuing the principle of legality. The authorities must function within legal parameters. Further-more, the existence of their power is not sufficient. The authorities must act reasonably and fairly and at the same time must take into account human rights considerations.

Third, the actions of the authorities are subject to the constant possi-bility of judicial control. More accurately, judicial control is possible at

M. C. Golumbic, *Fighting Terror Online.*
© Springer 2008

all stages, both before implementation of the means of prevention and enforcement, such as when applying for required warrants, and afterwards, such as in the aftermath of a direct or indirect attack.

2.1 The International Scene

2.1.1 Protection of the Right to Privacy

Modern treatment of the right to privacy at the international level is found in the Universal Declaration of Human Rights of 1948.[1] The guiding principle underlying the Declaration's approach is delineated in § 12, which states, "No one shall be subjected to arbitrary interference with his privacy, family, home or correspondence, nor to attacks upon his honour and reputation. Everyone has the right to the protection of the law against such interference or attacks." A large number of general international treaties expressly recognize the right to privacy, including the International Covenant on Civil and Political Rights (ICCPR)[2] and various UN treaties. The ICCPR explicitly states that "no one shall be subjected to arbitrary or unlawful interference with his privacy, home or correspondence, nor to unlawful attacks on his honour and reputation." It goes on to affirm that "everybody has the right to the protection of the law against such interference or attacks." At the regional level, there are conventions that have made the right to privacy a legally enforceable right, such as the European Convention of Human Rights and Fundamental Freedoms of 1950.[3] Using similar language to earlier declarations of rights, Article 8 of the Convention states that "everybody has the right to respect for his private and family life, his home and his correspondence." It goes on to say that "there shall be no interference by a public authority with the exercise of this right except such as in accordance with the law and is necessary in a democratic society in the interests of national security, public safety or the economic well-being of the country, for the prevention of disorder or crime, for the protection of health or morals, for the protection of the rights and freedoms of others." Following this convention, the European Human Rights Commission, the European Human Rights Court, and the Charter

---

[1] Universal Declaration of Human Rights (1948). http://www.hrweb.org/legal/udhr.html
[2] International Covenant on Civil and Political Rights (1966), Art. 17. http://www.hrweb.org/legal/ cpr.html
[3] European Convention of Human Rights & Fundamental Freedoms (1950), Art. 8.

of Fundamental Rights of the European Community were established, all of which aim to protect privacy and personal information.[4]

The recognition of the right to privacy in international law provides a foundation for the right to privacy as a basic human right. Most Western countries recognize the right to privacy at the level of national law as a constitutional right. More recent constitutions deal specifically with the right to privacy and the right to control personal information. Forty out of the fifty countries (including Israel) reviewed in the report of the Organization for Protection of Privacy (2000) demonstrated awareness and maintained clear rights regarding access to public documentation.[5] The protection granted at the international level and the recognition of the right to privacy in the national law of many countries indicate the importance of the right to privacy. This national and international awareness of the right to privacy is likely to have a direct influence on the checks and balances required in every situation in which this right may be compromised, particularly in the political climate created after the events of September 11 and in light of new technologies allowing unprecedented invasion of privacy.

2.1.2 International Regulation for Protection of Personal Data

The right to privacy also applies in specific cases concerning the right of the individual to prevent collection and processing of personal data concerning him. International protection of electronic data concerning the individual was established in the 1990 Convention for the Protection of Individuals with Regard to Automatic Processing of Personal Data.[6] This convention discusses personal data files and processing of data in the public sector and the private sector. It stipulates that the obtaining, processing, and storage of data must be conducted in accordance with the purposes for which it was collected. The data must be proper and relevant and must

---

[4] See: Charter of Fundamental Rights of the European Union, OJC 364.

[5] This is a survey conducted by the Center for Electronic Privacy in Washington and the International Center for Privacy in London. The report reviews the status of the right to privacy in some fifty countries by examining various areas of privacy, including data protection, wiretapping, data banks, identification systems, and freedom of information. http://www.privacyinternational.org/survey/phr2000/

[6] Convention for the Protection of Individuals with regard to the Automatic Processing of Personal Data (ETS No. 108, Strasbourg, 1981). At: http://conventions.coe.int/Treaty/EN/CadreListeTraites. htm (Report #108):

not deviate from those purposes. The holder of the data must guarantee its exactness, including the possibility of periodic correction and updating. However, at the same time, he must implement appropriate means of protection in order to safeguard the data from unauthorized access or modification. According to the convention, the means of protection of a person's privacy must be verified. Therefore, individuals whose details are included in the data must receive access to the information in such a way as to be able to determine the existence of the data file, its purpose, and the identity of the agency controlling the data. The individual must also have the possibility of receiving confirmation that the personal data is indeed stored, as well as confirmation of corrections or deletions. However, the convention recognizes exceptions that may be anchored in the national legislation of a country for purposes of protecting state security, public security, and the financial affairs of the State or for purposes of enforcing criminal law or defending the rights of others.[7]

This regulation, even though it is at the level of guidelines only and does not constitute normative law, is found in the United Nations Guidelines Concerning Computerized Personal Data Files.[8] This document only provides an outline, leaving the actual implementation of the regulation on automated personal data to each country's discretion. The following list of guidelines defines a series of principles in relation to a minimum standard of privacy at the national level:

- **Principle of lawfulness and fairness** – Information about persons should not be collected or processed in unfair or unlawful ways.
- **Accuracy** – Persons responsible for keeping the data have an obligation to conduct regular checks on the accuracy and relevance of the data recorded.
- **Purpose-specification** – The purpose for which the data is collected must be specified, legitimate and known, so that it will be possible to limit the storage to the area, time and capacity of use.
- **Access** – Anyone who offers proof of identity has the right to know whether information concerning him is being collected.
- **Non-discrimination** – Subject to cases of exceptions, data likely to give rise to discrimination, including information on racial or ethnic origin, color, sexual orientation, political opinions, religious,

---

[7] Yehonatan Bar-Sadeh, *Ha-Internet Vehamishpat Hamishari Hamekuvan*, The Internet and On-line Commercial Law 184–86 (Tel Aviv: Perlstein-Genosar, 1996).

[8] See: United Nations Guidelines Concerning Computerized Personal Data Files, adopted by the General Assembly on December 14, 1990.

philosophical and other beliefs, as well as membership in an association or trade union, should not be compiled.

- **Power to make exceptions** – Deviations from these guidelines may be authorized only if they are necessary to protect national security, public order, public health or morality, as well as the rights of others, provided that such deviations are expressly specified in a law and that their limits are expressly stated. With regard to the prohibition of discrimination and related data, additional safeguards are required within the limits prescribed by the International Bill of Human Rights.
- **Security** – Appropriate measures should be taken to protect data files against accidental loss or destruction or intentional tampering.
- **Supervision and sanctions** – The law of every country shall designate the authority that is to be responsible for supervising observance of the principles set forth above. In the event of a violation, criminal or other penalties should be sanctioned and appropriate remedies provided.
- **Trans-border data flows** – When the legislation of two or more countries concerned by a trans-border data flow offers comparable safeguards for the protection of privacy, information should be able to circulate as freely as within each of the territories concerned.
- **Application** – The principles should also be extended to data that is not stored by computerized means. The principles also apply to the data files in the possession of government agencies, subject to appropriate adjustments.[9]

Another international regulation on electronic data, although it has lesser importance, consists of the OECD Guidelines on the Protection of Privacy and Transborder Flows of Personal Data, Recommendation of the Council.[10] These guidelines set down the basic principles regarding collection, use, and disclosure of personal data and information. The guidelines recommend the following:[11]

- a restriction in local law to be imposed on collection of personal data;
- transparency with regard to the purposes of collection of the information and the intended uses of the information;
- disclosure of personal data only with the owner's consent;

---

[9] See: http://europa.eu.int/comm/internal_market/privacy/index_en.htm

[10] OECD, "Guidelines Governing the Protection of Privacy and Transborder Data Flows of Personal Data" Paris, 1981: http://www.oecd.org/document/18/0,2340,en_2649_34255_1815186_1_1_1_1,00.html

[11] Bar Sadeh, *supra* note 7, at 186–87.

- development of protections anchored in law;
- adoption of a policy of openness regarding personal data and safeguarding of the right of the individual to receive confirmation that data concerning him was collected, as well as the right to study the data, to verify that it is correct, and to protest data that is erroneous.

2.1.3 International Regulation of Encryption Products

On the international scene, we note a clear trend toward limiting (or even abolishing) control over encryption products and services.[12] In most countries of the Western world, it is now possible to freely create, use, and sell encryption products and encryption services. In line with the international report on encryption,[13] we can identify two policymaking bodies as the key players in rejecting limitations on encryption and developing a competitive, open market for encryption products: the European Union (EU) and the Organization for Economic Cooperation and Development (OECD).

2.1.4 International Regulation of Decryption Products

When an individual wants to protect his private information, he may choose to do so in a number of ways. In the home, digital protection mechanisms may be found in the form of a Pay TV decoder or in the form of a password upon entering a virtual shopping site or server. Each of these systems requires decryption in order to access and use the information.

International law regarding decryption has been enacted in three main areas: protection by means of legal frameworks that complement intellectual property rights (copyright), legislation related to conditional access to encrypted services, and legislation dealing with databases.

Copyright, in essence, provides its owner or holder with the right to control certain specified uses of his work. In recent years, various devices have been developed to offer technological protection of an individual's work. The law has chosen to recognize the right of the copyright holder to

---

[12] Cryptography & Liberty 1999/2000, E-commerce: A Guide to the Law of Electronic Business 63 (Daniel Tunkel & Stephen York eds., 2nd ed., 2000), available at http://www.gilc.org/crypto/crypto-survey-99.html and http://www2.epic.org/reports/crypto2000/ (12.12.01).
[13] Id.

use such devices in order to protect himself and his work in situations where others would like to circumvent those devices. The main legal arrangements that provide preferential status for technological means used in protecting copyright are the WIPO Copyright Treaty (WCT) and the WIPO Performances and Phonograms Treaty (WPPT).[14] These treaties are the work of the World Intellectual Property Organization, and underlying the organization's treaties are the Paris and Berne Conventions. They are aimed at updating the international protection given to copyright and related rights in the Internet age, taking into account developments in digital technology.

In accordance with the WCT, the creator-author of a work is entitled to legal protection regarding the distribution, commercial hiring, and public broadcast of his work over a network. Specific protection is given to systems for identifying and managing the author's work. Section 11 of the treaty provides protection against the circumvention of the technological measures that protect the author's rights.

2.2 The United States

2.2.1 Protection of the Right to Privacy

The right to privacy is protected in the US by the Fourth Amendment to the Constitution:

> The right of the people to be secure in their persons, houses, papers, and effects, against unreasonable searches and seizures, shall not be violated, and no warrants shall issue, but upon probable cause, supported by oath or affirmation, and particularly describing the place to be searched, and the persons or things to be seized.[15]

The Fourth Amendment restricts the American government's power to invade the privacy of the country's citizens and obliges the government not to infringe upon these rights without legal cause. It also sets a standard of "probable cause"[16] needed when the government wishes to intercept communications or obtain a search warrant, as carrying out actions of this kind may infringe upon the right to privacy of the person under surveillance.

---

[14] See: http://www.wipo.int/treaties/

[15] U.S. Const. Amend. IV.

[16] *See* United States v. Cavanagh, 807 F.2d 787 (9th Cir. 1987).

This protection is supported by a system of checks and balances established in the various laws and case law.

In October 2001, the US Patriot Act was promulgated. This Act reinforced and extended the surveillance powers of US domestic law enforcement authorities and international intelligence agencies. It is argued by some that this Act violates the system of checks and balances that was shaped in the 1970s, following the uncontrolled use of surveillance powers by various agencies (when over 10,000 citizens were placed under permanent surveillance, including Martin Luther King).

Under the new law, the court can oblige a service provider to deliver mail logs and addresses of a specific person if the government is able to present facts to show that the records are relevant to an investigation in progress. The question is whether this standard corresponds to the "probable cause" condition in the Fourth Amendment. There are those who argue that a distinction must be made between the collection of "content data" concerning a specific person and the collection of "numerical information" (e.g., numbers that the individual dialed or e-mail addresses with which he corresponded), for which the collection standard can be lower.

The new Act introduced modifications in some fifteen laws. Many of these amendments infringed upon the right to privacy in the electronic communications between citizens. The government may now be entitled to monitor innocent surfers if they keyed in a concept that "arouses suspicion" in an Internet search engine. All that the government has to do is to swear before a court that the act might lead to information relevant to an investigation in progress. The person whose computer is monitored does not necessarily have to be the subject of an investigation or the suspect in any crime.

Legal control of invasion of privacy by the enforcement agencies. American law recognizes four surveillance means: (1) interception of broadcasts, including wiretapping (interception orders); (2) search and seizure orders of actual objects (search warrants); (3) orders for locating to whom or from where a call was made (pen/trap orders); and (4) subpoena and court orders (for obtaining of information). The various warrants and orders require different levels of certainty and legal intervention in direct relation to the expected invasion of rights (such as privacy and freedom of speech).

Secret monitoring and interception. Intelligence agencies are not restricted in the employment of surveillance means outside the US. There is no legislation on the matter, apart from a directive of President Reagan, which is valid to this day.[17] The directive established that if a "United States person" is the subject of secret monitoring, then authorization must be received from the Attorney General, who has the power to decide whether there is probable cause that the target is a foreign agent.[18]

Two laws regulate surveillance within the US. One is the Federal Wiretap Act (1968),[19] which allows operation of surveillance and secret monitoring means through a court order after it has been demonstrated that there is probable cause that a crime has been committed, is being committed, or will be committed. The law contained a closed list of crimes for which a wiretap order can be given.[20] In the new law,[21] terror acts and offenses in line with the Computer Fraud and Abuse Act were added to the list.[22]

The Foreign Intelligence Surveillance Act of 1978 (FISA)[23] allowed the issuing of wiretapping orders by a special court for agents of a foreign power.[24] Here too, probable cause must be shown. However, in order to issue an order for someone who is a US person, it must be shown that the

---

[17] Exec. Order No. 12333, 3 C.F.R. 200 (1982), reprinted in 50 U.S.C. § 401 note.

[18] "United States person" means a citizen of the United States, an alien lawfully admitted for permanent residence (as defined in § 101(a)(20) of the Immigration and Nationality Act), an unincorporated association a substantial number of whose members are citizens of the United States or aliens lawfully admitted for permanent residence, or a corporation that is incorporated in the United States. The definition does not include a corporation that is associated with a foreign power, as defined in 50 U.S.C. § 1801(a)(1), (2), or (3). See 50 U.S.C. § 1801(i).

[19] The Omnibus Crime Control and Safe Streets Act of 1968, commonly known as the "wiretap law."

[20] 18 U.S.C. § 2516(1).

[21] US Patriot Act §§ 201–202.

[22] Computer Fraud and Abuse Act (CFAA), 18 USC § 1030.

[23] Pub. L. No. 95–511, 92 Stat. 1783, codified as 50 U.S.C. § 1801.

[24] See: United States Signals Intelligence Directive, July 27, 1993. The term 'agent of a foreign power' is defined as follows:

a. Any person, other than a U.S. person, who:

   (1) Acts in the United States as an officer or employee of a foreign power, or as a member of a group engaged in international terrorism or activities in preparation thereof;

   (2) Acts for, or on behalf of, a foreign power that engages in clandestine intelligence activities in the United States contrary to the interests of the United States, when the circumstances of such person's presence in the United States indicate that such person may engage in such activities in the United States, or when such person knowingly aids or abets any person in the conduct of such activities or knowingly conspires with any person to engage in such activities;

b. Any person, including a US person, who:

information is essential for national security, whereas for an individual who is not a US person, it must be shown that the information is related to national security. The definitions of an agent of a foreign power should be noted. According to this definition, the membership of a US citizen in a terror organization does not correspond to the definition of an "agent of a foreign power." To be classified as such an agent, the citizen must work to advance the terrorist objectives. The distinction lies in the protection that the First Amendment gives to American citizens, wherein membership and activity in a terror organization may be for the advancement of a specific idea, and the citizen cannot be systematically prevented from expressing his opinion. In emergencies (to protect life and limb), it is possible to implement surveillance means in pursuance of both laws, even without a court order.

Pen/Trap Orders.[25] The purpose of these orders is to find the location of outgoing or incoming calls. The courts approve the orders as long as they can provide relevant information for a criminal offense, and their discretion is mainly technical regarding the manner of filing the application. Section 216 of the new Act extended the authorization for tracing calls from line communications to electronic communications.[26] Section 214 of the new Act also extended the possibility of issuing a warrant within the counterintelligence framework (FISA) in cases of terror, but forbade opening an investigation of a citizen due to First Amendment considerations.[27]

The FBI's Carnivore system carries out similar activity on the Internet. The system is located at large data nodes and traces the source and the target of the messages transmitted over the Internet. The problem created is

---

(1) Knowingly engages in clandestine intelligence gathering activities for, or on behalf of, a foreign power, which activities involve or may involve a violation of the criminal statutes of the United States; or
(2) Pursuant to the direction of an intelligence service or network of a foreign power, knowingly engages in any other clandestine intelligence activities for, or on behalf of, such foreign power, which activities involve or are about to involve a violation of the criminal statutes of the United States; or
(3) Knowingly engages in sabotage or international terrorism, or activities that are in preparation, for, or on behalf of, a foreign power; or
(4) Knowingly aids or abets any person in the conduct of activities described in paragraphs 9.1.b.(1) through (3) or knowingly conspires with any person to engage in such activities.

[25] "Pen registers" are devices used to record telephone numbers that are dialed from a telephone; "trace devices" are used to determine where a telephone call originated.
[26] US Patriot Act §§ 216–202.
[27] *Id.* § 214.

that the system actually scans a very large quantity of data in order to find a specific piece of information for which the trace has been authorized. Another problem is that it is impossible to separate between the content and the data concerning the target, because they are transmitted together. Since the FBI does not specify the method of operation of the existing system, it is feared that such a system could collect not only information about the sender and receiver, but also information on the contents of the communication.

Search and seizure orders. Search warrants are issued by a judge when there is probable cause that a crime has been committed. At the time of or after execution of the search, the owner of the premises must be notified that a search was carried out. However, the new Act extends the power to secret searches in which the owner of the premises does not know that a search was carried out on his property/belongings. Search warrants also apply to seizing data that was received and stored by electronic means, including e-mail that has not yet been read.[28] The new Act allows interception, by search warrant, of line communication stored data, including voice mailboxes.[29] Under FISA, it is possible to carry out searches, without judicial control, with the authorization of the Attorney General.[30] Within the framework of this law, an investigation and search against a US citizen will not be carried out because of the freedom of speech protected by the First Amendment.

Receipt of information collected by access providers. Law enforcement agencies may request and receive information for purposes of carrying out investigations. Requesting the information is not subject to legal control. The new Act empowered law enforcement agencies to order and receive more extensive information from communications providers than in the past, including the time and duration of the telephone calls and Internet surfing, IP addresses, method of payment, and details of the person making the payment.[31] The authorities can order commercial records, such as data on transactions carried out by e-commerce and any non-content information related to subscribers.[32]

Section 217 of the new law allows for the study of information seized in computer trespasser communications.[33] The rationale for giving such

---

[28] 18 USC § 2703 (a) and (b).

[29] US Patriot Act, § 209.

[30] 50 USC § 1822.

[31] US Patriot Act, §§ 210, 211.

[32] 18 USC § 2703 (c).

[33] US Patriot Act § 217.

permission is that anyone hacking into a computer cannot expect privacy of his data. The new act allows the ISP to provide non-content data, without a warrant, voluntarily, to protect life and limb.[34]

The Communications Assistance for Law Enforcement Act (CALEA)[35] demands that communications companies adapt their systems to fulfill the control requirements of law enforcement agencies.

2.2.2 Protection of the Freedom of Speech

Issues about the preservation of freedom of speech have arisen in two contexts in the United States, with specific reference to encryption and decryption software. American law has viewed this issue from the perspective of the doctrine of "symbolic behavior" – a doctrine that was developed before the advent of digital technology. Case examples include public burning of the country's flag or draft cards in order to protest a government policy. The O'Brien case that came before the United States Supreme Court in the 1960s illustrates this point.[36] Paul David O'Brien and others publicly burned their draft cards, claiming that they did so in protest against the Vietnam War. O'Brien was arrested and placed on trial on the charge of burning his draft card in contravention of a 1965 law. The Supreme Court rejected the argument that all behavior or actions can be considered "speech" when carried out to express an idea or position. Moreover, the Court analyzed the situation in which action (behavior) and "speech" (in its First Amendment sense) were intertwined, and came to the conclusion "that when 'speech' and 'non-speech' elements are combined in the same course of conduct, a sufficient government interest in regulating the non-speech element can justify limitations on First Amendment freedoms." Thus in this type of case, an absolute standard of protection for freedom of speech need not be applied. Rather, a somewhat lower standard, known as "intermediate scrutiny," may be applied.[37] Chief

---

[34] *Id.* § 212.

[35] 18 U.S.C. § 2522.

[36] United States v. O'Brien, 391 U.S. 367 (1968).

[37] American legal decisions accept three standards for evaluating the extent of protection for freedom of speech. The highest standard, "strict scrutiny," is applied when the State prevents certain speech or the State discriminates between different types of speech based on their content. A lower standard, "intermediate scrutiny," is used by the courts when the limitation on speech is not based on its content; according to this standard, the court weighs the free speech rights of the speaker against the national interest in limiting that speech, with the weightier

Justice Warren established a number of conditions for public regulation, which, when present, justify the limitation of First Amendment rights:

1. The regulation is within the constitutional power of the government;
2. The regulation furthers some important governmental interest;
3. The regulation is not designed to restrict freedom of speech;
4. The incidental limitation on freedom of speech is not greater than necessary to promote the governmental interest.

In the O'Brien case, it was ruled that the law under discussion was not aimed at restricting freedom of speech, but rather at ensuring the effectiveness of the draft procedure (the governmental interest). Thus, O'Brien was not placed on trial for his opinions, but because of his behavior, which damaged the national interest.

The question arises as to whether it is possible to adopt the O'Brien ruling in the context of encryption software. American courts have not been consistent on this issue.

The first instance is known as the Karn case. Philip Karn, a programmer working on cellular technology, requested a permit to export source code for encryption algorithms on diskette. The same algorithms had already been published in book form prior to Karn's request to export them digitally.[38] Although the book had been declared by the Department of State and the Department of Commerce to be a freely exportable commodity, these same bodies ruled that the export of the code in digital form was prohibited under the regulations controlling the export of encryption software. Karn appealed the Administration's decision to the District Court in the District of Columbia.[39] His argument was that the diskette constituted "speech," particularly since the program code included programmer comments, which were not aimed at the computer running the program, but at a human reader looking at the source code and trying to understand it. As the issue was one of expression, the diskette should be protected by the freedom of speech protections under the First Amendment. On this basis, Karn argued that the prohibition against exporting the diskette was unconstitutional and thus null and void.

The court rejected his case. Although the court agreed that the protections offered by the First Amendment also apply to program code, it

interest winning. The third, and lowest, standard is called "rational basis;" here the speaker has to show that state regulation does not have any logical basis.
[38] *See* Bruce Schneier, APPLIED CRYPTOGRAPHY: PROTOCOLS, ALGORITHMS, AND SOURCE CODE in C 151–54 (2nd ed., New York, Wiley, 1996).
[39] Karn, Jr. v. U.S. Department of State, et al., 925 F.Supp. 1 (D.D.C. 1996).

ruled that when the restriction on speech is not content-based, but rather content-neutral, this implies that it is designed to restrict some other function that the speech serves, and is thus justified if it meets the conditions established in the O'Brien case.[40] In this case, the court ruled that the O'Brien test was met. The regulation of software exports is within the government's powers. Such regulation is not aimed at restricting freedom of speech, but at promoting an important governmental interest (here, to make it difficult for hostile states to interfere with the access of the United States government to information essential for national security); and the incidental limitation on freedom of speech is in appropriate measure.[41] It is important to note that Karn attempted to argue that the O'Brien test applied only to *behavior* that included in it speech. However, the court rejected that argument and ruled that the test applied to any form of expression.[42]

The Bernstein case led to a contrary decision in which freedom of speech had the upper hand. Daniel Bernstein, who was a mathematician researching cryptography at the University of Illinois in Chicago and the University of Berkeley in California, developed a novel encryption algorithm as part of his academic work. Bernstein wanted to distribute and export the program, which he called "Snuffle," accompanied by an article in which he analyzed and explained the program code. He also wished to share his findings at academic conferences, including some outside the United States. His intention was to disseminate his ideas within the scientific community throughout the world as part of the normal academic exchange of ideas and information. The Export Regulations prevented Bernstein from publishing or discussing his work – a move which, in his opinion, harmed his career and reputation. In 1996, Bernstein appealed to the United States District Court in California, claiming that his freedom of speech rights had been violated. Judge Marilyn Hall Patel ruled that the encryption program was a form of speech that was entitled to First Amendment Protection, because anything written in any language is, by

---

[40] *Id*. at 10.

[41] *Id*. at 11.

[42] The court rejected Karn's appeal for another, additional, reason – that the Arms Export Control Act established that decisions made by those authorized under that law were not subject to judicial review. Karn appealed the judgment, but the appeals court returned the case to the court of first instance (107 F.3d 923). The case was transferred because prior to consideration of the appeal, authority for issuing regulations restricting the export of encryption software was transferred from the Department of State to the Department of Commerce, and the latter was due to issue new regulations regarding that subject.

definition, a form of expression entitled to constitutional protection.[43] Further, Judge Patel ruled that the procedures for licensing encryption software constituted prior restraint on freedom of speech.[44] Finally, on this basis Judge Patel ruled that the Export Regulations were unconstitutional.[45]

The United States Court of Appeals for the Ninth Circuit, in a three-judge panel, upheld the ruling issued by Judge Patel,[46] but in a slightly more restrictive manner. The Export Administration Regulations were found to be unconstitutional, but not in an all-encompassing sense. An unconstitutional restriction can occur when the Administration imposes a restriction that prevents the flow of scientific ideas (whether by means of source code or some other means) without distinguishing between those and encryption products as commodities. In essence, the court ruled that not every program can be considered expressive speech. Only when "[c]ryptographers use source code to express their scientific ideas in [. . .] the same way that mathematicians use equations or economists use graphs" does the Constitution provide protection under the First Amendment.[47] Although the specific expression under discussion also includes a "non-speech element," the court noted that the O'Brien ruling does not have to be applied in all cases. In light of the prior restraint of freedom of speech, the court applied the highest standard in examining the extent of First Amendment protection.

In response to this decision, the United States Justice Department petitioned the court for a rehearing in the Bernstein case by an expanded panel. The court accepted the petition and withdrew the ruling by the three-judge panel.[48] However, changes in encryption export policy made the appeal hearing unnecessary and the case was returned to the District Court.

The third case dealing with the issue of encryption software and freedom of speech is the Junger case. Professor Peter Junger was a lecturer at Case Western Reserve University in Cleveland who was teaching a course in "Computing and the Law." Junger wrote a number of very basic encryption programs and wanted to place them on the course's Internet site in

---

[43] Bernstein v. United States Department of State, 922 F. Supp. 1426, 1435 (N.D. Cal. 1996).

[44] *Bernstein*, 945 F. Supp. at 1279.

[45] *Bernstein*, 974 F. Supp. 1288 (N.D. Cal. 1997).

[46] Bernstein v. United States Department of Justice, 176 F.3d 1132 (9th Cir. 1999).

[47] *Id.* at 1141, 1145; Judge Nelson, in a minority ruling, held that computer software cannot be considered speech.

[48] Bernstein v. United States Department of Justice, 192 F.3d 1308 (9th Cir. 1999).

order to show his students "how a computer works." However, he was
required to obtain an export license from the Department of Commerce
because under the International Traffic in Arms Regulations (ITAR), cryptographic computer software is considered a "munition."[49] His application
for the license was refused. Junger appealed to the Federal District Court
in Ohio, claiming that his First Amendment rights had been violated.[50]
The court accepted the position of the government and ruled that the
export of cryptographic software is not protected by the First Amendment,
even if encryption software occasionally includes a "speech" component.
The explanation was that software primarily provides functionality and
that expression is only a secondary aspect. Junger appealed to the Court
of Appeals for the Sixth Circuit,[51] which rejected the decision of the lower
court. In the appeal, the court ruled that the functional characteristics of
source code do not overshadow its expressive nature and that the O'Brien
ruling should be applied in such cases.

In two other cases, known as the DVD judgments, the courts in New
York and California ruled on the constitutionality of restrictions on the
publication and dissemination of software to break digital protection
mechanisms. Here, too, the courts were not of one mind in their judgments.

The factual background of the two cases is almost identical. The American film industry attempted to protect its investment in films in digital
format on DVD by means of a technology called Contents Scramble System (CSS), which is designed to prevent unlicensed viewing of the film or
of a copy. A Norwegian teenager wrote a program – DeCSS – that broke
this protection technology (according to the writer, with the aim of allowing the viewing of DVD films on computers operating under Linux). The
code for the decryption program was disseminated to universities through
the Internet, and the plaintiffs, who were interested in finding the most
effective way of cutting off its distribution, decided to sue the operators of
the websites that distributed the code.

In the first case, which was heard in New York, the main defendant
was a well-known hacker named Eric Corley, who placed a copy of the
decryption program on his website. The film companies sued him on the
basis of the explicit provisions of the Digital Millennium Copyright Act
(DMCA), which prohibits the publication or distribution of software that

[49] 15 C.F.R. § 734.2(b)(9).
[50] Junger v. Daley, United States Secretary of Commerce, 8 F.Supp.2d 708 (N.D. Ohio 1998).
[51] Junger v. Daley, United States Secretary of Commerce, 209 F.3d 481 (6th Cir. 2000).

can break digital protection mechanisms.[52] Judge Lewis A. Kaplan, sitting on the District Court,[53] ruled in favor of the film companies. Corley appealed, but the appeal was rejected.[54] One of Corley's main arguments was that applying the DMCA to the distribution of the decryption program violated his constitutional rights to freedom of speech, because it had already been ruled that computer code is a form of protected speech under the First Amendment. Both courts agreed that computer code does constitute protected speech.[55]

Judge Jon O. Newman, sitting on the Court of Appeals, agreed with the designation of computer code as protected speech and provided an interesting analogy. Just as musical notes, which constitute protected speech, are only comprehensible to musicians, so is decryption code comprehensible only to programmers.[56] The extent of the protection of speech is influenced by the nature of the program as a combination of a speech element and a functional, non-speech element.[57] Thus, the appropriate standard to be applied when determining the level of protection is that of "intermediate scrutiny," rather than the absolute standard. In other words, the appropriate test to apply in this instance is the O'Brien test.[58] Furthermore, the court ruled that the DMCA was not aimed at inhibiting freedom of speech, but at serving another important, constitutional interest, namely protecting copyright works and preventing "piracy." Therefore, the limitation on freedom of speech imposed by the law was proportionate and the DMCA prohibition on the distribution of DeCSS was constitutionally valid.[59]

Similar proceedings took place on the West Coast of the United States in a suit submitted by the DVD Copy Control Association (DVD CCA). DVD CCA is the holder of the rights to the DeCSS system and licenses the installation of the system to producers of DVD players. The suit named Andrew Bunner, who published the DeCSS program on his website, as the defendant. However, the decision of the California court was fundamentally different from that of the courts in New York. This time, freedom of speech won out. Under the Uniform Trade Secret Act, the lower

---

[52] 17 U.S.C. § 1201(a)(2), (b)(1).

[53] Universal City Studios, Inc. v. Reimerdes, 111 F.Supp.2d 294 (S.D.N.Y. 2000).

[54] Universal City Studios, Inc. v. Corley, 273 F.3d 429 (2nd Cir. 2001) (Universal II).

[55] *Universal City*, 111 F.Supp.2d, at 327.

[56] *Universal II*, 273 F.3d, at 445.

[57] Universal City, 111 F.Supp.2d, at 328–29.

[58] Universal City, 111 F.Supp.2d, at 329–30; Universal II, 273 F.3d, at 450.

[59] Universal City, 111 F.Supp.2d, at 330–33.

court issued an injunction against Bunner and others, ordering them not to publish or distribute DeCSS on the grounds that the decryption program contained CSS trade secrets. Bunner appealed to California's Appellate Court, which overturned the original ruling. Again, the court held that computer code constitutes protected speech under the First Amendment, but in this instance, the court did not adopt the O'Brien test and permitted publication of the code. The reasoning was as follows: In determining the balance between freedom of speech and trade secrets protection, which is not a constitutional protection, the court applies the highest standard, rather than the "intermediate scrutiny" standard, which corresponds to the O'Brien test.[60] It may be that the plaintiff's strategy undermined the claim, as the plaintiff only made a trade secrets argument against the alleged freedom of speech violation and did not present arguments based on copyright and DMCA infringement issues.[61]

2.2.3 American Regulation of Encryption Products

In recent years, the legal policy applying to encryption in the United States has undergone a fundamental change, with a move toward reducing restrictions and governmental control. Until 1996, the export of the means of encryption with a key length (strength) above 40 bits[62] was considered an export of munitions, and the control of trade in encryption means was carried out through the ITAR – International Traffic in Arms Regulations. Due to these severe restrictions and in order to respond to the needs of the software market, in 1993 the Administration proposed the idea of the Clipper Chip as a means of encryption. With control over licensing, the Administration would also retain the ability to decipher the Clipper Chip and to access any content encrypted therein. The idea was not successful. Opposition came from software companies, which were restricted in terms of software exports and competitively disadvantaged in world markets, as well as from human rights organizations and privacy advocates.

In November 1996, the Administration changed its position. The previous policy of a sweeping prohibition with limited exceptions was replaced

---

[60] DVD Copy Control Association v. Bunner, 113 Cal. Rptr. 2d 338, 350–51.
[61] Haim Ravia, "Pitzuah Ha-DVD [Cracking the DVD]." http://www.law.co.il/hebarticles/bunner.htm.
[62] For a technical explanation, see Chapter 4.

by a regime of export restrictions with exemptions.[63] Encryption means were now only considered as munitions if they were for military purposes. The Administration's goal was to support electronic commerce, protect global information infrastructures, protect privacy and intellectual property rights, and allow American companies to compete equally with their overseas counterparts. Authority for the control of encryption was transferred to the Bureau of Export Control (BXA), which is subject to the Department of Commerce. Encryption items were reclassified and transferred from the Munitions Control list to the Commerce Control list. The new regulations created a process by which the owner of means of encryption with a key length of up to 40 bits could have the product removed from the Commerce Control list after a single examination by the Bureau of Export Administration (BXA) and would then be exempt, in practice, from any export restrictions.[64] Similarly, it was possible to obtain an export license, but not removal from control, for encryption items that operated with 56-bit keys using DES technology[65] (or equivalent), subject to two conditions: first, a one-time examination of the product prior to export, and second, the existence of Key Escrow or Key Recovery technology to circumvent the encryption.[66]

The Administration is entitled to establish restrictions on export without the need for separate legislation, by virtue of emergency legislation.[67] A trend toward liberalization in the area of encryption exports from the United States, first evidenced by a series of permits issued in 1998 and 2000, which are described in detail below, continues today. However, closer examination of the regulations shows that political, economic and security considerations influence the possibilities of export to various countries.

As of this writing, there is no restriction on production or commerce of the means of encryption of any strength within the United States. Outside the United States, regulation is conducted by means of export regulations implemented by the BXA which is responsible for the administration

---

[63] Executive Order 13026 (November 15, 1996).

[64] 61 FR 68572 (1996), http://w3.access.gpo.gov/bxa/fedreg/ear_fedreg96.html#encryption1

[65] For a technical explanation of DES, see Chapter 4.

[66] These terms mean that a third party, who is not the owner of the encrypted information, will have the possibility of deciphering the information. The regulations define who can be the third party and the manner in which that party can be contacted in order to decipher the information.

[67] International Emergency Economic Power Act (IEEPA), codified as 50 U.S.C. § 1701; National Emergencies Act, codified as 50 U.S.C. § 1601; The Export Administration Act, codified as 50 U.S.C. § 2401.

of the export of encryption items.[68] The only blanket prohibition that remains in force is the export of means of encryption to states that support terrorism or their citizens.[69]

The first set of permits in the area of encryption exports from the United States was issued in 1998.[70] The most significant step in that year was the Administration's waiver of the blanket requirement for the means to decipher encrypted messages (back door). A further step was the strengthening of the technological defenses of financial institutions. Following are some of the changes implemented in that year:

- It is permitted to export, subject to license and after examination, technologies integrating means of encryption, to banks and financial institutions (including insurance companies), in 45 countries,[71] without the means of decipherment,[72] and without restriction on the strength of encryption. This permit is designed not for mass-marketing products, but for a limited market and for the purpose of carrying out secure transactions between financial institutions and their clients.
- An export permit is allowed for all encryption up to 56-bit strength after technical examination.
- It is permitted to export encryption to American subsidiaries or branches of American companies outside the United States.
- It is permitted to export encryption technologies for electronic commerce, under license, to 45 countries, on condition that the transactions are secured and that direct customer-to-customer communications are not carried out.
- A permit may be issued to export encryption commodities or software for health and medical uses to 45 countries without limitation on the strength of encryption, provided these are designated for end-users only.

---

[68] See Export Administration Regulations 740.13, 740.17, 742.15. http://www.bxa.doc.gov/Encryption/Default.htm.

[69] The states supporting terror, according to the American Government, are Syria, Iran, Iraq, Libya, Sudan, North Korea, and Cuba. Additional information relating to the policy of defining states as terror-supporting can be found in a document by the Congressional Research Service from March 2001, which deals with Terrorism and United States Foreign Policy: http://www.fas.org/irp/crs/IB95112.pdf. An additional explanation can be found at the State Department website: http://www.state.gov/www/global/terrorism/1999report/sponsor.html.

[70] See 63 FR 50516 (09.22.98), 63 FR 72156 (31.12.98), available at: http://www.bxa.doc.gov.

[71] See: Supplement No. 3 to (EAR), 15 C.F.R. Sections part 740. Today this Section no longer appears, since the restrictions are no longer unique to these countries.

[72] Key escrow or key recovery.

- Anyone who received an exemption from export restrictions for 40-bit encryption may upgrade the product to 56 bits.

Changes in 2000[73] led to a much more liberal situation regarding the export of encryption items, in particular to the countries of the European Union. After 2000, it became possible to export products and software that included encryption of any strength to companies, individuals, and non-governmental organizations without license and after a technical examination only. The mechanism of examination at an early stage and post-export reporting requirements provide the Administration with information regarding the strength and final destination of the encryption technology. These regulations facilitate business for communications companies and Internet service providers by allowing them broader use of encryption. Producers of short-wave radio technologies also benefit. Following are some of the key changes resulting from the legislation passed in 2000:

- After examination by the Administration, commodities or software with encryption of any strength may be exported to individuals, companies, and other non-governmental end-users. Similarly, it was now permissible to distribute encryption to all destinations, because uploading of an encryption item to the Internet no longer constituted "knowledge" of transfer of encryption to a terror-supporting state. The amendments allowed the exporter to simply notify the Administration that encryption means had been exported.[74]
- The regulations simplified export to countries of the European Union and additional countries in Europe, as well as Japan, Australia, and New Zealand.
- The regulations simplified the export of encryption items designed for short-wave radio technologies.
- It was now permissible to export encryption items to American companies outside the United States without prior technical examination. Encryption companies operating in the United States that employ foreign nationals no longer required an export license.

---

[73] See 65 FR 62600 (19.10.00), 65 FR 2492 (14.1.00), http://www.bxa.doc.gov/encryption/default. htm. See also the statement by the White House regarding the change in policy relating to the export of encryption: http://www.cdt.org/crypto/CESA/whousepress091699.shtml.

[74] In 2002, The Bureau of Export Administration (BXA) fined a software company, NeoPoint, for knowingly exporting 128 bit encryption software to South Korea without a license.

- It was now permissible to export Open Source Code subject to license, but the Administration had to be notified regarding the location of the code.[75]
- The regulations permitted communications companies and Internet service providers to integrate encryption in the services they provided.
- In most cases, there was an obligation to allow the BXA a one-time examination of the product.

These changes reduced the criticism of human rights and privacy organizations. The Center for Democracy and Technology[76] published two criteria by which the policy should be measured. The first is the extent to which the export regulations limit people around the world from using encryption technology in order to protect their privacy. The second is the freedom given to individuals to participate in the information economy without contravening US law. Based on these criteria, the Center raised certain criticisms of the new regulations, specifically in four areas:[77]

- The export permit was only granted for products that were "sold" (for payment), which means that there was no express permit for the free distribution of products containing encryption items, including products that were distributed online at no charge, such as secure Internet browsers.
- The broad definition of "government," which includes any state-owned or related organization or corporation, placed too high a demand on small businesses and individuals who would like to export strong encryption products to those bodies that are, unjustifiably, defined as governmental.
- The reporting and screening obligations that prevented strong encryption technologies from reaching terrorism-sponsoring states handicapped small and medium sized organizations and individuals from distributing these technologies. The reporting obligations regarding the destination of these technologies should take into account the fundamentally anonymous distribution of technologies through the Internet.

---

[75] Open Source Code is code in machine-readable language (See Computers Law, 5745–1995, Section 1, Definitions), which may be modified or from which encryption algorithms can be extracted. The term "open" means that the code is accessible to the public.

[76] http://www.cdt.org.

[77] See details of the Center's position in the letter to the BXA: http://www.cdt.org/crypto/admin/991206comments.shtml

- The restrictions on the export of encryption-related source code[78] affected the distribution of non-commercial source code designed for use and development by large numbers of users. Companies and organizations might be able to cope with the restrictions. However, the distribution of source code that was "not subject to any proprietary commercial agreement or restriction" created problems of enforcement, and the imposition of restrictions on everyone involved in developing the code was not practical.

2.2.4 American Regulation of Decryption Products

American regulation of copyright. The Digital Millennium Copyright Act (DMCA)[79] was passed by the United States Congress in 1998 as part of bringing American law into line with the 1996 WIPO Copyright Treaty.[80] This law is designed to prevent the circumvention of the technological measures that protect copyright works. The heart of the prohibition is in § 1201, which prohibits the circumvention of technological access measures:[81]

> No person shall circumvent a technological measure that effectively controls access to a work protected under this title.

In addition, the law prohibits the production, sale, provision, or distribution of any measure that, wholly or in part, is designed to circumvent technological measures that protect copyrighted materials:[82]

> No person shall manufacture, import, offer to the public, provide, or otherwise traffic in any technology, product, service, device, component, or part thereof, that is primarily designed or produced for the purpose of circumventing protection afforded by a technological measure that effectively protects a right of a copyright owner under this title in a work or a portion thereof.

Several questions may be asked about the extent of the prohibition: Does the law apply to the decryption of technological protections in general or only to those technological measures that protect works that are

---

[78] This refers mainly to encryption algorithms found in machine-readable source code.

[79] Pub. L. No. 105–304, 112 stat. 2860 (Oct. 28, 1998). http://www4.law.cornell.edu/uscode/17/ 1201.html.

[80] WIPO Copyright Treaty http://www.gseis.ucla.edu/iclp/wipo1.htm (1996).

[81] 17 U.S.C. § 1201(a)(1)(A).

[82] *Id.* § 1201(b)(1).

themselves protected by copyright law? The prohibition against deciphering technological protections is not limited to local (American) technologies, and therefore the deciphering of a protective technology that origi-
nates outside the United States is also an infringement of the law. The law
establishes a civil offense, but when the infringement has been carried out
for commercial advantage or private financial gain, then the infringement
is also a criminal offense.[83]

The law establishes a number of general protections, including the protection given to acts for research, examination, and evaluation of protection mechanisms:

- The law does not override the authority of the Administration, intelligence services, or law enforcement agencies to carry out activities
  for the purpose of investigation, protection, data protection, and intelligence gathering.[84]
- There is an exception that permits the circumvention of technological
  access protections for the purposes of research aimed at finding flaws
  and vulnerabilities in encryption technologies.[85] This exemption was
  inserted because of the concern of lawmakers that the prohibition of
  decryption would hamper the development of research into the flaws in
  existing technologies.[86]
- The "fair use" defense does not justify decryption in contravention of
  the provisions of this section.[87]

The first criminal prosecution under this law was against a Russian
citizen, Dmitri Sklyarov,[88] who developed a program that bypassed the
technological defenses of eBook, a technology that belongs to Adobe.
The program was developed for a Russian company called ElcomSoft,[89]
which was also named as a defendant. In December 2001, a plea bargain agreement was signed, and the prosecution agreed in effect to waive

---

[83] *Id.* § 1204(a).

[84] *Id.* § 1201(e).

[85] *Id.* § 1201(g).

[86] See the reports of the various Congressional committees: H.R. Rep. No. 105–551, pt. 2,
at 27 (1998); S. Rep. No. 105–190, at 15 (1998). One year after the law took effect,
the legislature demanded a report on whether the law actually had a negative effect on
encryption research. According to the report, it is still too early to draw conclusions. See:
http://www.loc.gov/copyright/reports/studies/dmca_report.html.

[87] 17 U.S.C. § 1201(c).

[88] For details of this case, see: http://www.eff.org/IP/DMCA/US_v_Elcomsoft/.

[89] See the company's website: www.elcomsoft.com.

Sklyarov's prosecution without a conviction being recorded.[90] The law has been interpreted in the context of a number of civil cases:

- Film companies sued to prevent websites from distributing the code that breaks the technological protections of DVD movies. Arguments regarding fair use and the unconstitutionality of the DMCA – in that it is restrictive of freedom of speech – were rejected by the initial court and the court of appeals.[91]
- In another case, also related to the question of DVD encryption, the California state courts dealt with the question of decryption in light of laws protecting trade secrets.[92] An interim decision removed the restraining order that prohibited distribution of the decryption code through websites. In this case, the court stated:

  > DVDCCA's [The Plaintiff] statutory right to protect its economically valuable trade secret is not an interest that is 'more fundamental' than the First Amendment right to freedom of speech or even on equal footing with the national security interests and other vital governmental interests that have previously been found insufficient to justify a prior restraint.[93]

- Another case related to a researcher who wanted to publish his research and was threatened with action under the DMCA. Professor Edward Felten cracked the protection technology of digital watermarks within the framework of a public competition sponsored by the developers of the protection scheme. Felten waived the prize with the intent of publishing the results of his research. However, he claimed, the music industry (the RIAA) threatened to sue him under the DMCA. Felten applied to the courts for a declarative judgment that would recognize his right to publish his research as a part of his right to freedom of speech. Although the District Court of New Jersey rejected his claim,[94] the music industry declared that it did not object to the publication.[95]

---

[90] Sklyarov testified against ElcomSoft. The court papers related to the plea bargain can be found on the Justice Department's website: http://www.usdoj.gov/usao/can/press/assets/applets/2001_12 _13_sklyarov.pdf

[91] See: Universal, *supra* note 53, at 346, aff'd Universal City Studios, Inc. v. Corley 2001 WL 1505495 (2nd Cir. 2001).

[92] Trade Secret Act, Cal. Civ. Code, § 3426.1 et. seq.

[93] DVD CCA v. Bunner 93 Cal. App. 4th 648 (2001).

[94] Felten v. RIAA (D.N.J.)

[95] http://www.wired.com/news/politics/0,1283,48726,00.html.

The trend that appears to be developing in American law is to prohibit the decryption of codes that protect works subject to copyright protection. It is not yet possible to draw any conclusions regarding the prohibition of decryption within the framework of trade secret protection.

2.3 The European Union

The European Union exists by virtue of the treaties that created it (Treaty of Rome, the Single European Act, and the Treaty of Maestricht). In creating these treaties, certain areas were placed from the start in the Union's sole jurisdiction, while a few areas were made subordinate to a kind of "parallel authority" and others were left to the exclusive authority of the individual countries.[96] Due to this division of powers, numerous qualifications appear in the different legislative items of the European Union concerning areas that were left outside the Union's jurisdiction, including: (1) issues of security and general state interests (excluding economic interests) and (2) the possibility of creating local legislation that will allow exceptions to the provisions in these cases.[97] Another aspect of the division of powers cited above can be found in the issue of enforcing legislation in the private sector in various countries. An example of this occurs in the context of imposing obligations on a private entity (such as service providers) to act in accordance with the demands of the enforcement authorities.

---

[96] Eran Lev, *Mishpat Hakehiliya He-Eropait* THE EUROPEAN COMMUNITY LAW 32–4 (Bursi, 1994).

[97] The European Union's legislation is made up of four types of legislation: The treaty (convention) is the supreme legislative item and can be compared to a law in a federal state, but it does not have direct application within the countries; regulations, which are considered the legislative item closest to normative legislation in a sovereign state and which constitute the only legislative item in the Union that is directly applicable; directives are an "original" creation in that they constitute the legislation that determines binding objectives, but leave the member countries to determine how to implement the objectives; and decisions, which are at the lowest level on the normative scale and resemble an individual order. The use of regulations is more accepted in those fields where the EU has clear jurisdiction and as a tool for bringing the domestic law of the member countries into line. See Lev, *supra* note 97, at 43–45.

2.3.1 Protection of the Right to Privacy

The EU Directive on Data Protection of 1995[98] required member countries to create laws for the private sector regarding the right to privacy in the areas of the collection, processing, storage, and transmission of personal data. In fact, the Directive allows for the free movement of electronic data between countries of the EU, while guaranteeing that individuals will be protected against possible abuses of the data.[99] The main points of the EU Directive on Data Protection are provided below. Personal data is defined in the Directive as any information relating to an identified person or a person who can be identified, either directly or indirectly, in particular by reference to an identification number or to one or more factors specific to his physical, physiological, mental, economic, cultural, or social identity.

The Directive defines several exceptions to the application of the regulation. Article 3(2) stipulates situations in which application to the entire data processing activity is qualified:

- In the course of an activity that falls outside the scope of EU law (in pursuance of the founding Treaty) and in any case of data processing operations concerning public security, defense, state security (including the economic well-being of the State), and the activities of the State in areas of criminal law. Within the framework of the treaties establishing the European Union, it was agreed that these laws would remain in the jurisdiction of the member countries; hence the reason for the exception.
- Processing of data by an individual in the course of a purely personal or household activity.

Domestic legislation in each country must be in line with the spirit of the Directive. However, Article 5 of the Directive expressly states that the countries may determine the precise conditions under which the processing of personal data is lawful.

---

[98] Directive 95/46/EC of the European Parliament and of the Council of October 24, 1995 on the protection of individuals with regard to the processing of personal data and on the free movement of such data. For the wording of the Directive, see: www.cdt.org/privacy/eudirective/EU_Directive_.html (last visit: 24.12.01).

[99] Bar-Sadeh, *supra* note 7, at 187.

In respecting the Directive, every business must meet several conditions. First, the company must guarantee that personal data collected from customers will be used in a legitimate and fair way for specific, explicit, and legal purposes and that the data will be kept updated and properly stored. Additionally, the business must notify the customers of the person responsible for the data and offer the customer the right to access and correct the data if necessary. The Directive emphasizes that once collected, the data will be used only with the customer's clear consent. Violation of these obligations entitles the customer to compensation. The penalties assigned to the business will be in accordance with the laws of the member state. Each country in the EU was also required to establish an independent supervisory body with a variety of powers, including investigation, monitoring, and blocking of businesses that collect personal data on their customers.

Regarding countries outside the EU, a prohibition exists on the transfer of personal data to countries not complying with the European data protection standard. The US and the European Union reached an agreement called the "Safe Harbor Framework," whereby American companies would be considered as meeting the standard. However, American companies are still subject to independent, non-governmental regulation, according to these seven basic principles: notice, choice, limitation of onward transfer, security, data integrity, access, and enforcement.[100]

Regarding countries other than the US, on December 4, 2001 the committee of member states approved a proposal for standard contractual articles to be adopted by data-processing organizations in countries outside the EU. This proposal was designed to prevent the refusal of onward data transfer due to non-compliance with the treaty requirements.[101]

Although the Directive dates from 1995, the relevant legislation in many countries came into force only in early 2000. Furthermore, legal proceedings were carried out in the European court against five countries because of their delay in adopting appropriate legislation in accordance with the schedule determined in the Directive (Luxembourg, Denmark, Ireland, Germany, and France). Of these countries, only the first three have since issued the required law, which came into force in July 2000. All of Germany's provinces except Sachsen and Bremen have passed the

---

[100] For a report on the implementation of the agreement with countries outside the EU, see http://ec.europa.eu/justice_home/fsj/privacy/thridcountries/index_en.htm (The incorrect spelling of /thridcountries/in the link is correct)
[101] Ibid.

required legislation, and France has modified its existing laws, but has not yet entered them into effect.[102]

The European Union's 1995 Directive for Protection of Personal Data created a comprehensive working framework in which other directives and decisions were adopted to expand the scope of application of the principles. Additional provisions were subsequently added in relation to the telecommunications market, dealing mainly with various obligations imposed on ISPs. These additional provisions will be discussed separately in the section on data collection by commercial organizations below.

After September 11, another convention was signed that affected law enforcement agencies and their relations with service providers: the International Convention on Cyber-crime. This convention originated with the European Union[103] and was opened for the signature of the European countries and other countries that participated in its formulation (Israel was not one of them). As of May 2006, 38 countries have signed the convention, including the US, Canada, South Africa, Montenegro, and Japan.[104]

The explanatory notes clarify that the aim of the convention is to realize three main objectives: (a) the harmonization of national criminal law to incorporate the field of cyber crime; (b) the creation of national procedural powers needed for the investigation and prosecution of cyber-crime and other offenses committed using computer systems; and (c) the establishment of an efficient framework for international cooperation.[105] In pursuit of these objectives, the covenant is made up of four chapters: (1) terms; (2) measures to be taken at the national level regarding substantive law and procedural law; (3) international cooperation; and (4) articles of reservations and their application. The convention defines eight offenses as substantive law including illegal access, illegal interception, system interference, misuse of devices, computer-related forgery, computer-related fraud, child pornography, and offenses related to infringements of copyright and related rights. Areas covered by procedural law apply to the basic offenses indicated above as well as to any offenses carried out by

---

[102] See: "Status of Implementation of Directive 95/46/ EC" http://ec.europa.eu/justice_home/fsj/privacy/law/implementation_en.htm

[103] The text of the convention can be found at: http://conventions.coe.int/Treaty/en/Treaties/Html/ 185.htm. The Council of Europe is an international organization that was founded in 1949. Today it has 45 member states, including countries of Eastern Europe.

[104] For monitoring of the countries signing the convention and their status, see: http://conventions.coe.int/Treaty/Commun/ChercheSig.asp?NT=185&CM=8&DF=10/5/2006 &CL=ENG

[105] http://conventions.coe.int/Treaty/en/Reports/Html/185.htm

using computer systems or by electronic means. The convention permits law enforcement authorities to search and seize computer data, collect traffic data in real time, and intercept content data.

The third chapter of the covenant defines provisions regarding traditional computer crimes and provisions for international cooperation, such as principles of extradition. The provisions deal with international assistance in two types of cases: (1) if there is a legal basis in the form of treaties or reciprocal legislation, then the existing agreement will be expanded to situations cited in the covenant; and (2) if there is no prior legal basis, then the provisions stipulated in the third chapter will apply. The chapter also contains a special provision on transborder access to stored computer data that does not require mutual assistance (with consent or where publicly available). A different special provision allows for the creation of a network designed to guarantee rapid assistance between signatory countries of the covenant.

Article 22 of the covenant deals with jurisdiction and provides criteria for determining jurisdiction over the criminal offenses stipulated in the covenant. The Article also allows the creation of additional jurisdictional bases within the framework of national law. In cases where a jurisdiction is established for more than one country, for instance in trans-border virus attacks on the Internet, the relevant countries shall consult with each other in order to determine in which country the trial will be held. Article 42 is another important article in the covenant, dealing with reservations and allowing several reservations (this is a closed list) in light of the nature and character of the covenant.

The field of telecommunications has been the subject of extensive legislation in the European Union as part of the effort toward free competition in this market. Within the scope of this legislation, the field of privacy was addressed in the EU Directive on Personal Data and Privacy in the Telecommunication Sector.[106] The directive imposed a broad range of obligations on service providers in order to guarantee the privacy of the users of communication means, including activities related to the Internet. The rules relate to fields, which, prior to these directives, fell between the cracks in the existing data protection laws. The rules of the directive apply to the processing of personal data in the telecommunications

---

[106] European Parliament and Council Directive 97/66/EC of December 15, 1997 concerning the processing of Personal Data and the Protection of Privacy in the Telecommunication Sector, OJL 24 (30.01.1998).

services available to the public in the EU, such as digital services (Integrated Services Digital Network – ISDN) and mobile telephones.

The Directive imposed restrictions on access to the information. For example, Caller ID technology must incorporate the possibility of blocking the transmitted number. Information collected during the course of a communication must be "cleansed" upon conclusion of the call. Subscribers are entitled to receive non-itemized bills. The provider must allow the subscriber to block automated calls coming from third parties. Subscriber directories must be limited to essential details only. Use of recorded advertising messages and faxes must be limited to subscribers who have given their consent.

As an extension of this directive, in July 2000 the Commission proposed a directive on data processing and protection of privacy in the electronic communications sector.[107] The proposal was submitted as part of an overall package, with the aim of encouraging electronic communications competition in the European market. The proposal suggested that a new directive replace the existing one of 1997 by extending the protection for communications of the individual to a broader technological and legal category of "electronic communications." The proposal replaced existing definitions of "telecommunication services and networks" with a new definition of "electronic communication services and networks." The proposal also added new definitions and protections for calls, connections, traffic data, and location data, the aim of which was to reinforce the consumer's right to privacy and provide the possibility of control in processing the various types of data.

These provisions would guarantee the protection of all the data related to Internet transmissions, ban unsolicited marketing by e-mail (spam) without prior consent by the "opt-in" method, and give mobile telephone users protection from wiretapping and immediate place location. The proposed directive also gives subscribers the opportunity to choose whether they wish to be entered in public directories. However, this proposed directive also gives the countries the possibility of limiting the provisions with security and enforcement need restrictions.[108]

This proposal was discussed in the European parliament, which has already submitted amendments to allow spam and to restrict the saving of service providers' information for law enforcement purposes. In pursuit of

---

[107] A Proposal for a Directive of the European Parliament and of the Council concerning the processing of Personal Data and the Protection of Privacy in the Electronic Communication Sector (2000) 385, OJC 365 (19.12.00).

[108] http://www.privacyinternational.org/survey/phr2000/overview.html#Heading12 (24.12.01)

the amendment, any surveillance and monitoring must be essential, appropriate, proportional, and time-limited. The means must be anchored in jurisprudence and approved on an individual basis by a relevant authority. This authority must be committed to the European Human Rights Convention and the ruling of the Human Rights Court. All these measures are in place to ensure that extensive or general electronic surveillance is not possible.[109]

EU Directive 1999/93/EC on Electronic Signatures[110] extended the provisions of the directive on personal data and imposed a supervisory and data storage obligation on certification service providers. These entities may collect personal data only directly from the data subject or after receipt of his explicit consent, and only in relation to what is required and obligatory for purposes of issuing the certification. The data must not be collected for other purposes (Article 8).

Liability of service providers. The Convention on Cyber-crime discussed above deals extensively with imposing obligations on service providers within the framework of procedural steps and powers granted to the enforcement authorities. This covenant gives a very broad definition to the term "service provider." The term is designed to include a wide category of individuals serving in a specific role in communications or in the processing of data in computer systems. According to this definition, both public and private entities that provide users with the ability to communicate with others are included.

Therefore, the question of whether the users create a closed group or whether the service is offered to the public, or whether the service is free of charge or provided for a fee, is irrelevant. A closed group can consist of employees in a private company who have access to the service by way of the company server. The definition also includes entities that store or process information in another way for the entities cited above or for the users. For instance, the definition includes "hosting" and "caching" services as well as Internet connection services. On the other hand, the definition of "service provider" does not include a content provider that does not also offer connection or data processing services.[111]

---

[109] For amendment of the directive in the framework of the European Parliament committees, see: http://www.privacyinternational.org/issues/cyber-crime/index.html#coe.(24.12.01).

[110] Directive 1999/93/EC of the European Parliament and of the Council of 13 December 1999 on a Community framework for electronic signatures, OJL 013 (19.01.00) pp. 0012–0020 http://europa.eu.int/smartapi/cgi/sga_doc?smartapi!celexapi!prod!CELEXnum doc&lg=en&numdoc=31999L0093&model=guichett.

[111] See the Covenant Explanatory Report: http://conventions.coe.int/Treaty/en/Reports/Html/185.htm

Within the framework of the procedural powers established by the Convention, obligations are imposed on the service providers. Section 18 of the Convention calls for legislation that requires the service providers to transmit customer information about the type of communication, as well as the subscriber's identity and geographic location. According to §§ 20–21, the service providers will also be obligated to provide information on content and communications in real time about the messages on their servers. Yet, the Convention makes it possible to demand that the service providers maintain the confidentiality of their consumers. One may wonder what effect this obligation of confidentially, on the one hand, and the obligation to provide information, on the other, will have on the commercial (and legal) relations between the service providers and their consumers.

2.3.2 EU Regulation of Encryption

In 1992, the European Union Commission established a committee to study the issue of information security and encryption. This initiative was part of a program that included a strategic working framework for information security; analysis of data protection needs; provision of solutions for those needs; specification, standardization, and verification of information security; integration of technological developments in the area of data protection; and integration of security functions in information systems.[112] The Commission published a number of reports and position papers,[113] which indicated an intention to develop a strategy to protect the internal market for encryption products and associated services. These position papers were translated into a number of directives, some of which are reviewed below.

One expression of the trend toward a free market for encryption products and encryption services can be found in the Directive on Electronic Signatures (Directive 1999/93/EC of the European Parliament and of the Council of December 13, 1999 on a Community framework for electronic signatures).[114] The issue of electronic signatures is closely connected with the area of encryption, because all certification processes are based on encryption keys. The definitions section of the Directive gives explicit and formal expression to concepts related to the encryption pro-

---

[112] Council Decision 92/242/EEC of March 31, 1992 in the field of information security.
[113] http://europa.eu.int/scadplus/leg/en/lvb/l24121.htm
[114] OJL 013 (19.01.2000) pp. 0012–0020

cess used in verifying electronic signatures. Examples of such techniques are signature-verification data (including codes or public encryption keys used to verify an electronic signature); signature-verification devices (configured software or hardware used to implement signature-verification data); and digital certificates, which are electronic attestations that link signature-verification data to a person and confirm that person's identity.

Sections 3–4 prescribe that the member states may not introduce restrictions on certification providers who wish to enter the market, nor can they establish any requirement for prior authorization as a prerequisite for receiving the necessary governmental permits. At the same time, voluntary programs may be introduced to enhance levels of certification service. All conditions related to such programs must be objective, transparent, proportionate, and non-discriminatory. Similarly, a supervisory system for service providers needs to be set up. Among other things, the Commission requires member states to report to the Commission on any national proposal to impose rules or restrictions on encryption products.

In 1997, the Organization for Economic Cooperation and Development (OECD)[115] published guidelines for encryption policy. These guidelines were directed mainly at governmental authorities, but were written with the expectation that they would stimulate interest from both the private and the public sector. Following are the principles listed in the document:

1. Encryption methods should be trustworthy in order to generate confidence in the use of communications systems.
2. Users should have the right to choose any encryption method, subject to applicable law.
3. Encryption methods should be developed in response to the needs and demands of the target audience.
4. Technical standards for encryption should be developed at the national and international level.
5. The fundamental right to privacy, including secrecy of communications and protection of personal information, should be respected in national encryption policies and in the implementation and use of the various methods.

---

[115] Organization for Economic Cooperation and Development. This is a forum established in 1961 and based in Paris. The organization includes the 29 developed nations (Israel is not a member). This international forum publishes guidelines on various topics related to economics and trade. These recommendations, although not officially binding, have a great deal of influence on the member states, as well as on states that are not members of this forum. See: http://www.oecd.org.

6. National encryption policy may permit legal access to the non-encrypted text (plaintext) and to encryption keys.
7. The responsibilities of bodies providing certification of encryption services or holding or accessing encryption keys need to be clearly stated.
8. Governments should cooperate to coordinate encryption policies. To this end, governments should remove, or avoid creating in the name of encryption policy, unjustifiable obstacles to trade.

The third principle is particularly noteworthy in that it stipulates the need for developing encryption methods based on the requirements of the free market. This principle states that research and development in encryption should be dictated by the needs, requirements, and responsibilities of individuals, businesses, and governments. As such, it ensures that developments keep pace with changing technologies, the demands of users, and market developments in general.

Along with the rejection of approaches based on local or national frameworks, most countries have rejected Key Escrow (Key Recovery) policies. These policies refer to the idea that users may use encryption in their systems, but a third – governmental – party would receive the keys to the code from encryption service providers. That government body would be responsible for providing the keys to the appropriate authorities when asked to do so.

This policy was adopted under French law in 1996, but the law was repealed in 1999. The British government also promoted this policy for a few years, and the United States tried to promote it, but was met with rejection on the part of the OECD. The United States also faced criticism from security experts who emphasized the problematic nature of a situation in which a central body holds the encryption key. The final rejection of this policy came in the Wassenaar agreements of December 1998 (see below). Today, only a few countries use this approach, and in the United States, the export restrictions that encouraged such an approach were repealed in January 2000.

As a result of the rejection of Key Escrow policies, a new approach was adopted by many countries: the demand for "lawful access" to encryption keys or message plaintext. Under this approach, individuals may be asked to reveal encryption keys to law enforcement authorities, and, if they refuse, they may be liable to criminal prosecution. Until the year 2000, only a few countries had enacted laws of this type. The OECD guidelines described above noted the principle of "access," but did not necessarily support it. The guidelines noted that national policy may permit legal access to the plaintext or encryption keys, but that this policy must respect the other principles in the organization's guidelines. This issue provoked sharp debate within the OECD until the organization finally decided not to support a global approach to "legal access."

In the context of the "lawful access" approach, consideration should be given to the right against self-incrimination, which is well founded and binding in many countries in the world. Underlying this right is the prohibition on governmental bodies to coerce an individual into giving testimony that may incriminate him. In this context, the argument exists that it is not possible to coerce individuals to reveal encryption keys or passwords that are not recorded elsewhere. In the United States, this argument has been raised in connection with the Fifth Amendment to the Constitution,[116] while in Europe the argument is based on the European Convention on Human Rights, which permits an individual to retain his right to remain silent.[117]

The EU has also made use of the Wassenaar Arrangement[118] in this context. The Arrangement refers to a series of agreements between 33 states to control the export of conventional arms and "dual use" (usable for both commercial and military purposes) goods and technologies. Under the heading of technologies, a number of encryption products that are considered "dual use" are included. The Wassenaar Arrangement is not a convention or type of legislation, but rather the exchange of opinions at the international level. Compliance of the participating states is a matter for each state's consideration and is carried out by means of legislation at the national level.

The main provisions of the Arrangement relate to the free export of encryption products based on key length, the easing of restrictions on the export of encrypted products in order to protect intellectual property rights, and licensing requirements for the export of encryption products not mentioned in the agreements. This is important in light of the fact that there is a significant loophole allowing for the free trade and distribution of non-tangible encryption assets by means of downloading from the Internet.[119]

---

[116] See, for example: Doe v United States, 487 US 201, 219 (1988) (Stevens J, dissenting) ("[a defendant] may in some cases be forced to surrender a key to a strongbox containing incriminating documents, but I do not believe he can be compelled to reveal the combination to his wall safe – by word or deed").

[117] http://www.fipr.org/ecomm99/ecommaud.html

[118] http://www.wassenaar.org

[119] CRYPTOGRAPHY & LIBERTY 1999/2000, *supra* note **12**

Within the framework of the international report mentioned above, countries are categorized according to the means of control applicable to trade in encryption products and services.[120] The report divides the countries that were investigated into three categories on the basis of how they control encryption. This categorization is designed to allow a world map of encryption policies to be drawn up for purposes of comparison. There are no accompanying sanctions to this categorization.

The "green" category includes countries that promote a policy permitting trade in encryption products without legal impediments, such as countries that have adopted the OECD guidelines. The "yellow" category applies to countries that have proposed state controls over encryption, including limitations on use or import, or those countries operating strictly within the provisions of the Wassenaar Arrangement. The last category – the one considered least desirable – is the "red" category, which includes countries that impose sweeping restrictions on encryption. Many countries do not fit exactly into one of these categories, in which case the report lists them as falling between the different categories.

2.3.3 EU Regulation of Copyright

On March 16, 2000, the EU ratified the two WIPO treaties (WCT and WPPT), noted above, which constituted the main legal arrangements providing preferential status for technological means used in protecting copyright. It also empowered the Commission to act on the issue of regulating copyright at various levels as a representative of the European Union. In line with this decision, the European Union could now become a party to the WIPO treaties for the regulation of copyright and related rights.

The following year, the European Parliament passed Council Directive 2001/29/EC, which sought to harmonize certain aspects of copyright and related rights in the information society.[121] The aim of this directive was to adopt legislation regarding copyright and related rights in a manner that reflected technological developments in the Information Age. It also introduced the WIPO treaties into EU law. The Directive deals with three main areas: copyright, public broadcast and transmission rights, and distribution rights.

---

[120] *Id.*
[121] OJL 167 (22.06.2001).

First, the member states are required to provide legal protection against the circumvention of effective technological means that protect copyrighted works. This legal protection relates to preparatory acts, such as the production, import, distribution, sale, or provision of services that circumvent technological protections. Another provision relates to rights-management information included in the copyrighted work, that is, information about the copyright owner or the terms and conditions for use of the work. The Directive also provides legal protection for the technological measures taken by copyright holders to prevent illegal modification or circumvention.[122]

A second means of protecting copyrighted material and encryption methods, as well as restricting decryption, is the legal protection given to technological services that operate by restricting access to content. A 1998 European Directive established a uniform legal framework for proceeding against devices or services that provide unlicensed access to copyright-protected services, such as television, radio, cable transmissions, satellite transmissions, and electronic publications. The framework applies when such services are provided to the public through subscriptions or payment for viewing.[123]

In this context, an "illicit device" is defined as any equipment or software designed to give access to a protected service (Article 2(e)) in an intelligible form without the authorization of the service provider. "Infringing activities" include the manufacture, import, distribution, sale, rental, or possession for commercial purposes of illicit devices. The installation, maintenance, or replacement for commercial purposes of illicit devices is also prohibited. Furthermore, the member countries of the European Union are prohibited from restricting the protections afforded to protected services that originate in another member country and from restricting the free movement of conditional access devices, except those defined as illicit. The member countries were required to enact internal legislation in line with the provisions of the Directive by June 28, 2000.[124]

---

[122] http://europa.eu.int/scadplus/leg/en/lvb/l26053.htm.

[123] See: Directive 98/84/EC of the European Parliament and of the Council of 20 November 1998 on the legal protection of services based on, or consisting of, conditional access, OJL 320, 28/11/1998 P. 0054–0057. http://europa.eu.int/smartapi/cgi/sga_doc? smartapi!celexapi!prod!CELEXnum doc&lg=EN&numdoc=31998L0084&model=guichett

[124] http://europa.eu.int/scadplus/leg/en/lvb/l26050.htm

England, for example, has implemented the Directive within the framework of its Copyright, Designs and Patents Act 1988 (CDPA).[125]

Note that, in spite of the broad definitions found in the Directive, it is not clear whether passwords obtained illicitly fall into the category of "illicit devices," because a password is not necessarily a device nor, is it software designed to provide access to the protected service. [126]

A third means by which encryption is protected – in that there exists a legal restraint on decryption – is by means of the protection given to databases. The European Union's directive on the legal protection of databases is Directive 96/9/EC of the European Parliament and of the Council of March 11, 1996.[127] The Directive created, within a framework separate from traditional copyright laws, a new intellectual property right regarding databases. This new right is based on the substantial investment (measured either qualitatively or quantitatively) in obtaining or verifying the material in the databases, as opposed to the criteria of creativity and originality required for protection under copyright law.

The Directive prohibits the extraction or other use of information in such amounts as would be deemed qualitatively or quantitatively significant (Article 7(1)). It also establishes a prohibition against extracting data from a database and reusing such data in any manner or in any forum. As such, it creates an effective prohibition against breaking the encryption of such material. The fair use protections in respect of this right have been narrowed. Permitted uses include the extraction for private use of data from a non-electronic database for purposes of teaching or scientific research and for purposes connected with public security and/or judicial procedure (Article 9). This last protection – a specific exception aimed at public security needs – permits the extraction of data from a database for security purposes. Such an act will not be deemed an infringement of the intellectual property rights that exist with respect to that database. These rights are in addition to the copyright protections applicable to the database as a result of originality of design or arrangement of the data.[128]

---

[125] See §§ 297A-298, and an explanation in: ALAI 2001 Congress Questionnaire, http://www.law.columbia.edu/conferences/2001/Reports/uk_ic_en.doc.

[126] CRYPTOGRAPHY & LIBERTY 1999/2000, *supra* note 12, at 71.

[127] See: OJL 77 (27.03.96).

[128] http://europa.eu.int/servlet/portail/RenderServlet?search=DocNumber&lg=en&nb_docs=25&domain=Legislation&coll=&in_force=NO&an_doc=1996&nu_doc=9&type_doc=Directive

2.4 Other Countries

2.4.1 Britain

A comprehensive law called the Anti-terrorism, Crime and Security Act 2001 was promulgated by the British Parliament[129] in order to amend the anti-terrorism law passed in the year 2000 and to lay down additional provisions on terror and security. The law extended the prevention and enforcement powers of the government authorities, allowed storage of traffic data for a long period of time, and determined the provisions for disclosure of information to the authorities. The law also deals with a variety of areas, including immigration; xenophobic crimes; weapons of mass destruction, poisons, and the nuclear industry; security in the field of aviation; bribery and extortion; and the handling of property and funds of terrorist organizations.

British regulation of encryption. In May 2000, a law implementing the European Directive on Electronic Signatures (99/93/EC) came into effect. Under the Cryptography Service Provider and the Electronic Communication Act 2000, British law established the registration process for encryption service providers and establishes legal recognition of electronic signatures. In line with the provisions of the law, the Secretary of State is required to establish and operate a Register of Encryption Service Providers.[130] Companies that are entitled to registration are those that provide services such as public key verification for individuals, administration of encryption keys, timestamping services for electronic signatures, and storage of encryption keys. Although the law does not provide specific criteria for registration approval, it does list the necessary details to be submitted upon application, including the proposed technology, the identity of the applicant for registration, and the means by which the applicant will offer the technology to the public. This law explicitly rejects the Key Escrow approach – whereby a secret government body would collect the keys – in favor of keeping a register of service providers that is open to the public.

An important aspect of the law is the fact that the register is voluntary. As a result, any encryption service provider can trade in the open market

---

[129] http://www.hmso.gov.uk/acts/acts2001/20010024.htm (last visit: 23.12.01)

[130] Encryption service providers are defined in Section 6 of the law: "Any service which is provided to the senders or recipients of electronic communication, or to those storing electronic data, and is designed to facilitate the use of cryptographic techniques."

without reference to his absence from the public register or concern for the fact that his application for registration was rejected. At the same time, it should be remembered that the significance of the register's being public is the fact that it is open to public scrutiny and examination, and thus serves as a tool to assist in selection and review in this area.[131]

British regulation of copyright. The British Copyright, Designs and Patents Act 1988 established, in §§ 296–297, a prohibition against the development, import, sale, rental, or advertisement of any device or measure aimed at circumventing the protection against copying a protected work. The broad terms of the prohibition include the publication of information that assists in carrying out acts designed to circumvent such protections. In addition, the law also prohibited unlicensed decryption.[132]

One of the tests of this law came in the case of Mars UK v Teknowledge Ltd[133], which dealt with a claim for breach of confidentiality by means of reverse engineering of a device that held encrypted data. In line with the requirements developed in a previous judgment,[134] the court found that the encrypted information itself was not confidential, considering that the device (Cashflow) was available to the public, and that there were no special circumstances suggesting an obligation to maintain confidentiality on the part of the respondent. It is important to note that the judgment made clear that encryption itself does not make encrypted material confidential in the absence of any other relationship between the source and the decoder.[135]

British regulation of decryption. Another important item of British legislation is the Regulation of Investigatory Powers Act 2000. The legislation obliges service providers to disclose encryption keys or location of the keys. However, the object of the legislation is to guarantee a balance between the right of enforcement authorities to interfere in electronic transmissions and the protection of business interests and individual rights. The regulations deal with four different actions: (1) interception of transmissions; (2) close surveillance; (3) human data sources; and (4) disclosure of encrypted information. It is possible to carry out an action against an individual or an organization only upon receipt of a corresponding order, which must be based on proof that the action is for the sake

---

[131] See CRYPTOGRAPHY & LIBERTY 1999/2000, *supra* note 12, at 59.

[132] *Id.* at 70.

[133] Mars UK v. Teknowledge Ltd [2000] FSR 138.

[134] Coco v. AN Clark [1969] RPC 41.

[135] CRYPTOGRAPHY & LIBERTY 1999/2000, *supra* note 12, at 63–64.

of national security, to prevent a serious crime, or to guarantee British economic interests.

In such a case, the service provider would be required to grant access to transmissions and to disclose any protected information (namely, any encrypted information), both for transmissions still in progress and for information stored with the service provider. Some maintain that the legality of this law is doubtful in light of the European Human Rights Convention, which was assimilated into British law in the Human Rights Act 1998.[136]

2.4.2 Canada

In December 2001, most sections of the C-36 Anti-Terrorism Bill, influenced significantly by the events of September 11, were enacted into law.[137] This legislation introduced several new sections into the criminal code that were designed to fight terror. The new offenses extended the existing law to include a group of situations considered to be indicative of terrorist activity, such as offenses against international notables or UN personnel, offenses that involved the use of explosives or other lethal devices, and offenses relating to the funding of terror acts.[138]

The objectives of the Canadian law were to regulate personal, financial, and medical data privacy, and to create reliable and uniform regulation for e-commerce and electronic documents. The law was designed to give the individual personal data protection rights. It defines the methods by which organizations can collect and use personal data, and outlines the rights of the individual to access and modify the data. The law requires that businesses disclose the object of the data collection and receive consent before collecting the data. The law does not exempt non-Canadian companies from abiding by the law. This category includes entities that are not Canadian, but collect data in Canada or on Canadian citizens.

---

[136] *Id*. at 60.

[137] The Canadian parliament passed the legislation on November 28, 2001 and was submitted for approval by the Senate, after which the law returned to Parliament for implementation. http://www.canadianliberty.bc.ca/.(24.12.01)

[138] http://www.parl.gc.ca/37/1/parlbus/chambus/house/bills/government/C-36/C-36_1/901 68bE. html

The law also indicated that its objective was to adapt the legal situation in Canada to meet European requirements. As of January 2003, all organizations have become subject to the laws' dictates.

2.4.3 Australia

In Australia, the Privacy Protection Law of 2000[139] relates to the management of company information systems and seeks to protect personal and sensitive electronic data. The law, which came into force in December 2000, sets two basic requirements:

1. Protection of personal data from misuse and unauthorized access, modification, or disclosure.
2. Destruction or permanent de-identification of unnecessary information.

According to the principle of NPP4, "reasonable steps" must be taken to safeguard the physical security of the data, the security of the computer systems and networks, and to establish secure communications. Appropriate training of the staff or workers is also required.

After the events of September 11, several cyber crime laws were legislated in Australia, including a 10-year prison sentence for cyber crimes. The laws dealt with "standard" computer offenses and offenses by means of computer, such as unauthorized use. The cyber crime laws also permitted investigations for "pure" criminal cases, such as murder and fraud. The laws included seven new "high-tech" offenses that covered hackers, prevention of service attacks, vandalism at sites, dissemination of viruses, and the use of computers in offenses such as harassment, fraud, and sabotage. Since 2000, the law has been periodically reviewed, but its substance has remained the same as when it was originally enacted.

---

[139] http://www.cfa.org.au/Issues/Privacy.

Chapter 3
The Legal Framework in Israel

3.1 The Right to Privacy

In Israel, the right to privacy is a basic constitutional right anchored in the Basic Law: Human Dignity and Liberty.[1] This constitutional status guarantees that any violation thereof must be done in accordance with the terms of the restriction clause. As such, the violation must be committed legally and must correspond to the values of the State of Israel as a Jewish and democratic state. It must have an appropriate object and be effectively functional only to the required extent.[2] In light of the importance of the right to privacy, the Knesset saw fit to anchor the protection of privacy in law even prior to its constitutional anchoring. In 1981, the Privacy Protection Law 5741–1981 was promulgated.[3] According to this law, intentional violation of the right to privacy is a criminal offense.[4] This designation sets a high behavioral standard. The rationale for this serious ruling is that those who violate a person's privacy should not be deterred by a financial penalty alone.[5] If the violation of privacy was committed in circumstances under which a legal, moral, social, or professional obligation to do so was imposed on the person responsible, then he would be protected from civil or criminal action.[6] Using the Privacy Protection Law, the Knesset sought to provide a legal solution for a rising increase in the infringement of privacy. This decision came in the wake of the spread of mass means of communication; the development of technological devices

---

[1] Section 7 of the Basic Law: Human Dignity and Liberty.

[2] Section 8 of the Basic Law: Human Dignity and Liberty.

[3] Privacy Protection Law, 5741–1981, Book of Laws 5741 128.

[4] Section 5 of the Privacy Protection Law.

[5] Knesset Proceedings 20 (5741–1981) 1770 (M.K. Amnon Linn).

[6] Section 18(2) (b) of the Privacy Protection Law.

M. C. Golumbic, *Fighting Terror Online.*
© Springer 2008

allowing wiretapping, remote tracking, and detection; and the expansion of the collection and centralization of information in the hands of public and private entities.[7]

However, the Privacy Protection Law does not discuss the subject of data collection in computer centers, assuming that this subject would be regulated by separate legislation.[8] Also worthy of note is the fact that automated data collection is not listed in § 2 of the Law as a possible violation of privacy. Of course, the list of areas covered by the law is an open list that can be amended by the courts. In 1981, the lawmakers predicted that constant technological development would likely create new methods of violation that could not have been foreseen at the time of promulgation of the law.[9] Only in Chapter 2 of the Privacy Protection Law, which deals with the protection of databank privacy, did the Knesset deal with a limited aspect of infringement of the right to privacy due to technological development. This section discusses the potential for serious harm to the individual if the personal data stored in computers is not protected, as well as the legal regulations in Israel that permit the invasion of privacy through search and seizure and secret monitoring.

3.1.1 Search and Seizure

Search and seizure actions are legally permitted in order to protect state security interests and the right to life, as well as to facilitate crime prevention and punishment. However, these goals may have a negative effect on the right to privacy and the economic interests of various organizations. Several cases have addressed these issues.

In the John Doe Affair, it was ruled that the use of administrative arrest should be considered in light of the restrictive clause in the Basic Law: Human Dignity and Liberty.[10] It was concluded that a balance must be found between the defense of State security and the basic human right to freedom.

In the Public Committee Against Torture case, which dealt with the General Security Service investigator's right to interrogate suspects of terror acts with physical means, it was ruled that the violation of the

---

[7] Privacy Protection Draft Law, 5780–1980, DL 206.

[8] *Id.*

[9] *Id.*

[10] CMC 3514/97, pp. 6/97 John Doe v. the State of Israel, Tak. Supr. 97 (2) 176, 177.

liberty of the person under interrogation is allowed only if it is for a proper purpose and not beyond what is necessary.[11] This ruling took into consideration the State's wish to protect the dignity and liberty of the person being interrogated.[12] The requirement of immediacy exists if there is a concrete and real risk of occurrence of the event (such as in the event of a "ticking bomb").

Search and seizure of material in computer systems. The Computers Law added "computer material," "computer," and "output" to the definition of "belongings" in the Definitions section of the Criminal Procedure Ordinance (CPO).[13] In the explanatory notes to the draft law, it states that authorization for the penetration of a specific computer would be issued according to search laws. Since the search provisions in the Criminal Procedure Ordinance did not include the search of computer material, they were amended so that the search of data or software on or belonging to a computer was also possible. Furthermore, an addition to § 32 of the Criminal Procedure Ordinance (§ 32(b)) was passed, whereby a court warrant is required for the seizure of computer material belonging to an institution in order to prevent disruptions in the operation of the business or public entity. A "search and penetration of computer material" warrant can be issued by a judge in accordance with §§ 23, 23a, and 43 of the Criminal Procedure Ordinance (Search Warrants, Penetration of Computer Material, and Order to Obtain Article, respectively). Receipt of data through a search of the communications between computers is not considered secret monitoring (§ 32a(c) of the Criminal Procedure Ordinance).

In the Netvision vs. IDF case, the court obliged the service provider, Netvision, to furnish the security forces with material collected in its computers from the e-mail transmissions of four of its customers.[14] Netvision was required to furnish the said material in accordance with §§ 23 and 43 of the Criminal Procedure Ordinance. The State Attorney indicated that a warrant for seizure of e-mail in a service provider's computers would be issued only on the basis of the Secret Monitoring Law. In response, the court indicated that an article seized by way of a search without a lawful warrant is still admissible as evidence. Justice Even Ari restated the decision delivered in the Nahmias Case, in which Supreme Court

---

[11] HCJ 5100/94, 4054/95 The Public Committee Against Torture v. the State of Israel, Decision 53 (4) 817.

[12] *The Public Committee Against Torture, supra* note 11, at 834–835 (Supreme Court President Barak).

[13] Criminal Procedure Ordinance (Arrest and Search) [New Version], 5729–1969.

[14] MC 090868/00 Netvision Ltd. v. Israel Defense Forces & others (hereafter: Netvision Case).

President Barak ruled that "this new regulation strikes a between the right to privacy and the infringement thereof, between inadmissibility of evidence and protection of the public interest."[15] Thus, the court ruled that the material stored in Netvision's computers could be seized even if the procedure that led to its storage was later found to be improper.

Other legal search and seizure regulations. It is possible to close an Internet site under the provisions of § 5 of the Prevention of Terror Ordinance, which stipulates that any property of a terrorist organization, including property on the site of the organization's activities, in the possession of a member of the organization, or that served in the organization's activities, will be confiscated. Section 6 of the ordinance allows the Police Inspector General to close a place of activity of a terrorist organization.[16]

Section 74 of the Emergency Defense Regulations allows the confiscation of articles when it is suspected that an offense was committed in regard to them or that they may serve as proof of an offense. Section 99 allows the seizure of any banned publication; §§ 100–101 allow the search of any device used for printing. Section 120 allows confiscation of the property of any person who transgressed these regulations.[17]

The definition of an investigatory action in § 1 of the Legal Assistance Between States Law includes a search of premises and seizure of proof or an object (including computer material) and inspection thereof. Article 2(a) defines legal assistance, among others, as search and seizure actions related to a civil or criminal case. Sections 29–30 contain an object seizure application procedure.[18]

3.1.2 Secret Monitoring in Israeli Law

The development of wiretapping and surveillance means and the ever-increasing use of electronic monitoring have given rise to new legal questions regarding modern technology. There is an urgent need to solve the problems deriving from secret monitoring, among them the ease of use of listening devices, the ignorance of the injured party of the fact that his

---

[15] CA 1302/92 IP v. Nahmias, Decision 49 (3) 309 (hereafter: Nahmias Case).
[16] Prevention of Terrorism Ordinance, 5708–1948.
[17] Defense Regulations (Emergency), 1945.
[18] Legal Assistance between States Law, 5758–1998.

calls are being monitored, the difficulty of detecting existing monitoring, and the limitation on protecting oneself against secret monitoring.

A first secret monitoring draft law was submitted as early as 1962.[19] The explanatory stated that "it is necessary to guarantee, by a criminal provision, that the privacy of the call will not be violated by secret monitoring." The draft law did not become legislation, and another draft law was formulated 16 years later,[20] providing the basis for the law promulgated by the Knesset.[21] The object of the draft law was to find the right balance between an individual's right to privacy and the general right for protection from the use of modern technological wiretapping means.[22] The law was designed to guarantee that the invasion of a person's privacy by secret monitoring would be permitted only in cases where public-social interests take precedence over the right to privacy.

In formulating the Secret Monitoring Law, the legislators based themselves on the American model in which there is an explicit distinction between secret monitoring, which is prohibited, and monitoring and recording a call with the consent of one of the parties, which is permitted. It was considered that if this distinction did not constitute a criminal violation of individual rights in the USA (the "bastion of safeguarding of the individual's rights"), then it should be applied in Israel as well.[23]

According to the Secret Monitoring Law, monitoring of someone else's call, recording or copying thereof, by a device and without the agreement of *either* of the parties to the call, is considered secret monitoring and is legally prohibited.[24] By extension, if one of the parties to the call agreed to the wiretap, then it does not constitute secret monitoring.[25] However,

---

[19] Prevention of Secret Monitoring Draft Law, 5723–1962, DL 5723/62.

[20] Penal Code Draft Law (Secret Monitoring), 5738–1978, DL 5738/301.

[21] Secret Monitoring Law, 5739–1979, Law 5739/118 (hereafter: Secret Monitoring Law).

[22] CA 48/87 Eitan Chahnover v. IP, Decision 41 (3) 581, 587–88 (hereafter: Chahnover Case).

[23] Knesset Proceedings 5735–1975, 3974.

[24] See definition of "monitoring" and "secret monitoring" in § 1 of the Secret Monitoring Law. For interpretation of the decision and definitions of "call," "party to a call," and "call of others," see: *Chahnover, supra* note 21, at 591–96. In this case, the Supreme Court ruled that "anyone who says things by a communications means that reaches or can reach the ears of many, makes all those who hear it parties to his call... When the person initiating the call says what he has to say in such a way that others can listen, he assumes the risk that others whom he did not intend to listen to the call will hear it. Like a person who shouts to his friend in public, he cannot expect his words to remain secret."

[25] In the explanatory notes to § 1 of the Penal Code Bill (Secret Monitoring) 5738–1978, it states: "It is proposed not to forbid the monitoring of a call when one of the parties to the call agreed to this monitoring." The assumption is that the said consent removes the call from the definition as a call that was intended only to be made personally.

monitoring a call and recording it for purposes of committing an offense or a damaging act constitutes prohibited secret monitoring, even if one of the parties to the call gave his consent.[26] In the Zuberi case, it was ruled that a man can be considered a "party to a call" even if he only listens, provided that the other directs the message directly to the listener.[27]

We can see that one area dealt with by the Secret Monitoring Law is the actual prohibition of secret monitoring. The Law also restricts the application of the prohibition, stipulating two exceptions: one relates to cases where monitoring is permitted a priori without the need for authorization; the second applies to cases where permission is accorded for secret monitoring that is not in the public domain. When a call is made *in the public domain*, monitoring of it by a person authorized to listen is not considered unlawful secret monitoring.[28] While such monitoring requires authorization, the law does not stipulate concrete authorization.[29] However, it seems that the authorization must be by name, must relate to a specific matter, and in as far as possible must be restricted in time and place. [30]

The law places more serious substantive and procedural obstacles for monitoring in the private domain.[31] As previously stated, secret monitoring is allowed only for two purposes: for the protection of state security or for the prevention of crimes and the detection of criminals. The authorization may be given only to a state authority. Secret monitoring for state security purposes can be executed with a written authorization from the Prime Minister or the Minister of Defense,[32] and in urgent cases with an authorization from the head of the General Security Service or the Head of

---

[26] Section 3 of the Secret Monitoring Law.

[27] CA 1497/92 IP v. Zuberi, Decision 47 (4) 177, 193.

[28] Section 8 of the Secret Monitoring Law. The "public domain" is defined as "a place where a reasonable person could expect his calls to be heard without his consent, and also a place in which a detainee or prisoner is held at that time." Authorization to carry out such secret monitoring will be given by the head of a security authority for reasons of state security or by a police officer for the prevention of crimes and the detection of criminals (§§ 8(1)(a) and (b) of the Secret Monitoring Law, respectively). For an explanation of this concept, see: CF 546/78 Bank Kupat Am Ltd. v. Hendels, Decision 34 (3) 57; Rehearing of Civil Appeal 13/80 Hendels v. Bank Kupat Am, Decision 35 (2) 785.

[29] See in this matter: Regulation 2 of the Secret Monitoring Regulations 5746–1986, Collection of regulations 5746/1118.

[30] Alex Stein: "Ha-Azanat Seter Umaakavim Electroniyim Nistarim Ke-emtza'im Lekiduma shel Hakira Pelilit Uvithonit" (Secret Monitoring and Secret Electronic Traces as Means of Advancement of a Criminal and Security Investigation), Mishpatim 14 (5745–1985) 527, 543–46 (hereafter: Stein).

[31] *Id*. at 533.

[32] Definition of "Minister" in §§ 1 and 4 of the Secret Monitoring Law.

the Intelligence Branch in the IDF General Staff.[33] Secret monitoring for the prevention of crimes and the detection of criminals requires authorization from the President or Vice-President of the District Court.[34] In urgent cases, an authorization from the Israel Police Inspector-General suffices.[35]

Secret monitoring without a lawful authorization constitutes a criminal offense, for which a penal sanction can be imposed in pursuance of a provision of § 2(a) of the Secret Monitoring Law.[36] The section sets down two further criminal offenses: use of information and placing of devices.[37] Section 2(2) of the Protection of Privacy Law stipulates that "legally prohibited monitoring" constitutes an infringement of privacy.[38] However, while secret monitoring constitutes a tort according to the Privacy Protection Law,[39] it does not constitute a criminal offense under the provisions of that law.[40]

Proof obtained by means of secret monitoring, contrary to the provisions of the Secret Monitoring Law, will generally be inadmissible in any judiciary procedure, unless the required conditions for admission of the evidence were fulfilled.[41] Prior to amendment of the Secret Monitoring Law in 1995,[42] § 13 constituted a mandatory provision that left no room

---

[33] Definition of "Defense Authority" in §§ 1 and 5 of the Secret Monitoring Law.

[34] Section 6(a) of the Secret Monitoring Law.

[35] Section 7 of the Secret Monitoring Law.

[36] The nature of the Secret Monitoring Law as a criminal law is also shown by the original name of the draft law – the Penal Code Draft Law (Secret Monitoring, 5738–1988). See also: Uri Rosen: "Al Ha'azanat Seter ve-al Pegi'a Bepratiut Beha'azanat Seter" (On secret monitoring and invasion of privacy in secret monitoring), Mishpatim 17 (5747–1987) 146, 148–49 (hereafter: Rosen).

[37] Sections 2(b) and (c), respectively. On the parallel application of the Secret Monitoring Law and the Privacy Protection Law on these acts, see: on criminal and civil liability for one act, in pursuance of the Secret Monitoring Law and the Protection of Privacy Law, Rosen, *supra* note 36, at 160–62.

[38] Privacy Protection Law. The widespread opinion today gives priority to the regulation stipulated in the Secret Monitoring Law over that stipulated in the Privacy Protection Law.

[39] Section 4 of the Privacy Protection Law stipulates that "infringement of privacy is a civil wrong." On criminal and civil liability for one act, in pursuance of the Secret Monitoring Law and the Protection of Privacy Law, see: Rosen, *supra* note 36, at 160–169.

[40] Section 5 of the Privacy Protection Law sets down a list of infringements of privacy that constitute a criminal offense; however, it does not specify an alternative in pursuance of § 2 (2) of the Privacy Protection Law. Accordingly, in matters constituting secret monitoring, legal action will not be taken in pursuance of the Privacy Protection Law. See for this matter the Badir Case and Rosen, *supra* note 36, at 156–160.

[41] Section 13(a) of the Secret Monitoring Law.

[42] The Secret Monitoring Law (Amendment), 5795–1995, Book of Laws 1995, 180. In the past, § 13(a) of the Secret Monitoring Law included inadmissibility. The amendment of the provision in § 13 was designed to create checks and balances between the need to detect truth

for the discretion of the court regarding admissibility of the evidence. Today, the court may, in certain circumstances and according to its discretion, admit information gathered through secret monitoring as evidence even if it was obtained unlawfully.[43]

Authorization for carrying out secret monitoring, both for the purposes of state security and for the prevention of criminal offenses, is issued for a period not exceeding 3 months and can be extended again.[44] Such an authorization would seem to seriously infringe upon the right to privacy, even more so than the infringement deriving from a search warrant. A search is carried out on a one-time basis and with the suspect's knowledge, whereas secret monitoring continues over time, is performed without the suspect's knowledge, and may even infringe upon the privacy of innocent third parties.

While it is the legislature that has established the desirable balance between the conflicting interests in the Secret Monitoring Law, it is the Court's role to deal with the interpretation of the law and the concrete implementation of the balance of interests. As already mentioned, secret monitoring for crime prevention requires a prior court authorization.[45] Implementation of the regulation in the Secret Monitoring Law depends on how the courts have interpreted the expressions "in the public domain" and "in the private domain." Verbal explanation of these expressions does not appear to be necessary, and the guiding policy considerations must adapt themselves to technological developments. An objective-proprietary distinction can be proposed, determining that a private area in which any person can enter and stay is considered the public domain. Given that the Secret Monitoring Law is intended to protect people rather than property, this distinction may be irrelevant.[46] A broader outlook that protects the privacy of a person rather than the privacy of a place may be preferable. A subjective criterion might also be proposed, based on the expectations of the parties.[47]

---

and do justice, on the one hand, and to prevent infringement of the rights of the individual, on the other. It gave discretion to the court to admit evidence even if it was obtained through a transgression of the Secret Monitoring Law. See: The Secret Monitoring Draft Law (Amendment), 5794–1994, DL 5754–1994.

[43] For the legal situation prior to amendment of the Secret Monitoring Law, see: CA 2286/91 IP v. Iluz, Decision 45 (4) 289, 304. For the legal situation after the amendment, see: *Nahmias Case, supra* note 15, at 325–326, 357–358.

[44] Sections 4(c) and 6(e) of the Secret Monitoring Law.

[45] Section 6(a) of the Secret Monitoring Law.

[46] The distinction is based on Stein's article, *supra* note 30, at 533–35, 556.

[47] Id. at 533, 535.

From this, we may conclude that technological progress in the communications market gives rise to legal doubts. It is up to the courts to decide the outcome of borderline cases, using the existing legal regulations.[48] However, it seems that changes occurring in technology lead simultaneously to modifications of the legal tools. For instance, the Secret Monitoring Law was amended in light of the development of wireless communications.[49] The Secret Monitoring Law initially defined a "call" as "by speech or another communication means." Over the years, the question has arisen as to whether monitoring a call transmitted "over the ether" also falls within the purview of the prohibition. In the not-so-distant past, the monitoring of a wireless telephone call did not constitute an offense according to the Secret Monitoring Law. Today, there is no doubt that listening to a cellular telephone conversation is subject to the regulations stipulated in the Secret Monitoring Law.

A "call" is also defined as including "communications between computers." Therefore, the recording of information from communications between computers is considered monitoring, and in the absence of agreement of the parties to the call, it is considered secret monitoring, which constitutes a criminal offense.[50] The monitoring of communications between computers does not constitute "penetration of computer material," as indicated in § 4 of the Computers Law.[51]

This gives rise to the question of whether use of the Internet for conversation purposes is open to tracing and monitoring by investigative and security agencies. On the one hand, Internet users "expect safeguarding of their privacy," because the public Internet demands strict compliance with the provisions of the Secret Monitoring Law in the interests of encouraging free use of modern computer communications. On the other hand, preventing the infringement of privacy in a dialogue is not always possible, even if desirable, when it opposes another vital public interest.[52]

---

[48] See *Chahnover Case*, and CA 5424/96 IP v. Dov Tal, Tak. Supr. 96 (3) 88; CA (Tel Aviv) 1770/97 State of Israel v. Laufer, Tak. Dis. 98 (2) 2377

[49] See Secret Monitoring Draft Law (Amendment no. 3) (Prohibition on monitoring a wireless telephone call), 5755–1994, DL 5755, at 122; Secret Monitoring Draft Law (Amendment no. 4) (Prohibition on monitoring a wireless telephone call and increasing penalties), 5755–1994, DL 5755, at 123.

[50] Section 2 of the Secret Monitoring Law establishes the legal liability of prohibited monitoring.

[51] Computers Law, 5755–1995, Book of Laws 366. See in this context: Miguel Deutch: "Hakikat Mahshevim Be-Yisrael" (Computer Legislation in Israel), Iyunei Mishpat 22 (5759–1999) 427, 440–42.

[52] See the *Netvision Case*.

In the Badir case, it was determined that communications between computers includes, among others, communications to a voice mailbox that is managed by computer.[53] Hence, the monitoring of a voice message on an answering machine without the consent of the person leaving or receiving the message is considered secret monitoring. Therefore, it seems that the protection of the Secret Monitoring Law extends to various methods of computer communication, but the secrecy of the conversation itself is not necessarily protected.

In the Netvision case,[54] the question arose as to what extent the investigative and security agencies are entitled to penetrate e-mail messages of an Israeli Internet subscriber. Another concern was whether the security agencies may require Internet access providers to carry out prolonged track and trace activities for purposes of investigation. According to the current legal situation, as reflected in the position of the State Attorney, e-mail that was already transmitted to the Internet access provider can be seized by order of a Magistrates Court under the provisions of the Criminal Procedure Ordinance (Arrest and Search).[55] For e-mail not yet transmitted to its destination, the seizure will be effected by an order of the President or Vice-President of the District Court in accordance with the Secret Monitoring Law.[56]

In the El Mazri case, it was ruled that secret monitoring outside the borders of the State of Israel does not have to be authorized by the President of the Court.[57] In the Assaf case, the High Court ruled on the lawfulness of monitoring calls between an inhabitant of southern Lebanon and an inhabitant of Israel, when the monitoring was carried out simultaneously in Israel and in Lebanon.[58] The appellant's defense counsel argued that the Secret Monitoring Law does not apply to southern Lebanon and that in any case, there is no court in Israel empowered to authorize secret monitoring of this kind. In order to monitor a call, it was ruled that the Secret Monitoring Law does not require authorization for monitoring from both parties to the call and that it suffices to have authorization from one of

[53] See the *Badir Case*.
[54] See the *Netvision Case*.
[55] Criminal Procedure Ordinance (Arrest and Search) [New Version], 5729–1969, Laws 284.
[56] Haim Ravia "Lo Yado Ha-aruka shel Hahok" (Not the long arm of the law) (June 2000). http://www.law.co.il/showarticles.php?d=h&article=40.
[57] CF 4211/91 IP v. El Mazri, Decision 47 (5) 624. For criticism of the decision in the El Mazri case, see: Yehonatan Ginat "Hatehula Hahutz-territorialit shel Zehuyot Ha-adam Ugevulotav shel Hok Ha'azanat Seter" (The extraterritorial application of human rights and the limits of the Secret Monitoring Law) Haperkalit 42 (5755–1995) 518.
[58] CF 568/99 Assaf v. IP, Tak. Supr. 2001 (2) 242, 246.

them. Therefore, even if the monitoring of a telephone call in Lebanon is inadmissible as evidence, it can be concluded that the monitoring of the call in Israel, in which the conversations of both parties to the call are recorded, is admissible as evidence.

Criticism of this ruling countered that in light of the Basic Law: Man's Dignity and Liberty, the correct interpretation of the Secret Monitoring Law is its application to every person wherever he is, whether he is on or outside Israeli territory. If the basic premise is protection of a person's privacy, then the Secret Monitoring Law prohibits the monitoring of a conversation in a place where the party of the call expects, and is entitled to expect, privacy. This legitimate expectation does not disappear with a change in the place of the call. Hence, the criterion of the location of the communications means that being monitored should not take precedence over the criterion of infringement of privacy. Therefore, the Secret Monitoring Law applies extraterritorially, and secret monitoring in the Occupied Territories requires a prior court authorization for carrying out of the monitoring.

Mutual assistance between countries in carrying out secret monitoring. The objective of the Legal Assistance Between Countries Law is to regulate the different principles, methods, and actions employed by the State of Israel to grant legal assistance to other countries. Additionally, the Law regulates the provisions for applications by the State of Israel to another country for the receipt of legal assistance.[59]

Secret monitoring is included in the definition of "investigatory action," which is listed among the actions that may be carried out within the framework of legal assistance.[60] While the legal assistance regulated in the law is granted both in civil and in criminal cases, the application of another country for secret monitoring in Israel is carried out only with respect to criminal cases. The competent authority in Israel will apply to a district court for authorization to carry out secret monitoring if one of the terms stipulated in § 31(2) of the Legal Assistance Between Countries Law exists.[61] Application for legal assistance from a foreign country is

---

[59] As indicated in the explanatory notes to the Legal Assistance Between Countries Draft Law 5957–1997, DL 5957–1997 at 131.

[60] See §§ 1 and 2 of the Legal Assistance Between Countries Law. Section 5 of the Legal Assistance Between Countries Law stipulates an escape provision, allowing refusal of the application of another country, if the legal assistance is liable to prejudice the security of the State of Israel or the public welfare.

[61] Authorization for secret monitoring will be granted only if requested for an offense, which in pursuance of the laws of the applicant country, carries a sentence of more than three years imprisonment; or in the case of an offense for which secret monitoring would be authorized if

not a routine matter, and appropriate arguments and reasons must be submitted as to why the court should accept the application. The applicant must convince the court that the evidence is required for the procedure before the court. The applicant must also explain why he himself will not apply to the foreign country for the evidence, particularly in the case of available documents required in a civil procedure.[62]

Secret monitoring and personal privacy. The Secret Monitoring Law does not protect the individual from electronic intrusion and tracing; rather, the law is designed to protect the individual from intrusion into his private calls.[63] The Privacy Protection Law applies to the electronic tracing of a person's movements[64] and recognizes the need of the defense authorities to act in order to safeguard social and public interests. However, in contrast to the Secret Monitoring Law, the Privacy Protection Law does not include *positive authorization* to carry out the electronic tracking of a person's movements.[65] Instead, the Law permits the infringement of privacy by giving an *exemption* to the security and investigatory authorities, or those employed by them, who acted "reasonably in the scope of their functions and for the purpose of their performance."[66]

The legality of infringement of a person's privacy must take into account the legitimate aims of a criminal or security investigation.[67] Material obtained within the framework of unlawful monitoring cannot serve as evidence in court, except with the injured party's consent, unless the court authorized the use for reasons that are on record.[68] The question arises as to whether the provision of § 2(1) of the Privacy Protection Law prohibits online tracking of the activities of Internet users. Surfing the Internet leaves "tracks" that allow the creation of a personal profile about

---

the offense were committed in Israel; or if the secret monitoring is for the purpose of confiscation of assets, as stipulated in § 6 of the Legal Assistance Between Countries Law.

[62] CMC (Jerusalem) 2168/99 Prof. Malvina v. Dr. Wolf, Tak. Dis. 99 (3), 29742, 29743.

[63] Stein, *supra* note 30, at 528–29.

[64] The Privacy Protection Law defines infringement of privacy as "detection or tracking of a person, liable to harass him . . ." (§ 2(1)). Section 5 of the Privacy Protection Law also stipulates that infringement of privacy may be a criminal offense in circumstances in which the public interest is threatened.

[65] For a criticism, see: Stein, *supra* note 30, at 555–56.

[66] Section 19(b) of the Privacy Protection Law. The "balance formula" adopted by the Privacy Protection Law differs from and is more complex than that adopted by the Secret Monitoring Law, because it contains more legally protected interests.

[67] Stein, *supra* note 30, at 555.

[68] Section 32 of the Privacy Protection Law.

the user. This capability increases the fear of infringement of the user's right to privacy.[69]

3.2 Freedom of Speech

Freedom of speech is recognized in Israel as a fundamental principle, although it is not mentioned explicitly in the Basic Laws. In a number of decisions, the Supreme Court has ruled that the right of Human Dignity is to be read into the Basic Law. Therefore, it may be assumed that the limitation on speech will be examined in light of the near certainty test and that this is likely to be read into the Violation of Rights clause. Israeli courts have not yet been asked to deal with this question.

3.2.1 Liability of Service Providers

Today, in Israeli law, there is no specific regulation in legislation or in case law regarding the question of Internet Service Provider (ISP) liability for the content or nature of the information published on servers.[70] On the question of ISP liability for infringement of privacy, the opinion was expressed, in the context of cookies, that everyone is aware of the potential infringement of their privacy through cookies, but few take any action to prevent the infringement; therefore, the liability for the infringement of privacy cannot be placed on the ISP. It is inconceivable that the public would permit the infringement of privacy through cookies, while at the same time demanding financial compensation for the use of cookies. On the other hand, in the case of dissemination of defamation on an Internet site, the ISP must be obliged to divulge the identity of the distributor if requested to do so by the court, despite the infringement of privacy. Moreover, distributors of harmful content (e.g., defamation) should not

---

[69] Haim Ravia "Pratiut Bareshet" (Privacy in the Internet) (four parts –Jan.–Feb. 1999).
http://www.law.co.il/showarticles.php?d=h&article=45;
http://www.law.co.il/showarticles.php?d=h&article=46;
http://www.law.co.il/showarticles.php?d=h&article=47;
http://www.law.co.il/showarticles.php?d=h&article=48
[70] Brian Negan, "Liability for Illegal Material in Internet Laws." (March 1998).
http://www.itpolicy.gov.il/vadat_inter_gov/docs/illegal.rtf

be entitled to receive legal protection preventing the disclosure of their identity due to reasons of privacy.[71]

Existing legislation regarding cellular service providers and cable broadcast franchise-holders may provide ideas for an appropriate law in relation to ISP liability. In pursuance of § 13 of the Bezeq Law, 5742–1982,[72] when requested to do so by the Minister of Defense or the Minister of Internal Security, a licensee for the operation of Bezeq activities or for the provision of Bezeq services or satellite transmissions must allocate resources to the security forces. Further, there are special articles in the license for carrying out Bezeq services, which set down specific instructions in relation to the licensee's obligation toward the defense system.[73] In § 6(25) of the Bezeq Law there is a list of broadcasts that the license-holder for cable broadcasts or satellite broadcasts is forbidden to broadcast.

In actual practice, ISPs confirm that they will keep digital evidence of any offense, from the time of receipt of such a request, to be presented later to the police when required.[74] The existence of such a practice strengthens the need for legislation regarding ISP liability. The goal of this legislation would be to impose identical liability on all ISP providers and to prevent the phenomenon of the slippery slope. Such a slippery slope might occur if Netvision, for instance, were to carry out further infringements of privacy (due to its demonstrated willingness to violate the customers' privacy by storing digital evidence) before being asked to do so by the police and without a legal basis.

In Israel, the existing law does not explicitly regulate the liability of ISPs for the harmful or defamatory statements of third parties. In specific fields, liability applies to traditional intermediate agencies (that are not Internet providers) through explicit legal provisions (for instance, the Copyright Law) or as a function of case law (for instance, patent laws). The current legal situation concerning ISPs is unclear and brings into question the constitutionality of some of the existing regulations.[75]

---

[71] Aviv Ayalon & Yehonatan Bar Sadeh, "Maakav Kiberneti" (Cybernetic Monitoring). http://www.psakdin.co.il/fileprint.asp?FileName=/Ip/Public/art_balx.htm&Highlight= מעקב20%קיברנטי|טנרביי20%בקעמ

[72] Bezeq Law, 5742–1982, Book of Laws 218.

[73] For instance, in his lecture, Adv. Sharon Keren of Cellcom noted that § 48 of Cellcom's license orders the absolute allocation of resources to the defense system. Section 66(a) of the Cellcom license obliges the company to allocate special services to the defense system.

[74] As indicated by Mr. Ariel Pisetzky, CEO of Information Security at Netvision, at the Shefayim Conference.

[75] See, for instance, the position of Gad Barzilai, "Mercaz neged Periferia: Dinei "Meniat

In Israeli law, there is a series of prohibitions on terror acts,[76] as well as on indirect assistance to terror acts,[77] but the application of these prohibitions to the digital medium is not clear. For instance, in the Defense Regulations there is an obligation of censorship, by the military censor, of information intended for publication.[78] The law defines the term "publication" very broadly as: "to distribute, disseminate, deliver, announce, or make available to all persons."[79] It is not clear whether an Internet site on which a forum is conducted is subject to the law for the offenses committed by the surfers participating in the forum. The ambiguity of the law is also evident in the case of a provider who allows access to terrorist sites. Another prohibition in the Regulations is the provision of printing services to a banned association.[80] Again, here too, it is unclear as to whether this section is applicable to Internet sites.

The Prevention of Terror Ordinance, 5748–1948, reflects the policy that the fight against terror calls for a fight against accompanying infrastructures. For instance, § 1 of the Ordinance broadly defines "membership in a terrorist organization" to include anyone publishing propaganda for the organization. Section 2 defines "activity of a terrorist organization" to include propaganda speech at a public meeting or on the radio by a terrorist organization. Section 4 defines "support of a terrorist organization" to include oral or written publications[81] of sympathy or call for support of the terrorist organization; possession of propaganda material for such an organization; support with money or monetary equivalent; or the placing of an object or physical area at the disposal of the terrorist organization. Here too, there is a lack of clarity. It is not clear as to whether these prohibitions apply only to the content provider (the actual speaker) or also to the provider of the advertising platform. Nonetheless, the courts have

---

Terror" Kepolitica" (Center versus Periphery: "Terror Prevention" Laws as politics), Pelilim 8 (5760–2002) 229.

[76] See, in particular, Prevention of Terrorism Ordinance, 5708–1948.

[77] See, for instance, Defense Regulations (Emergency), 1945, in particular, §§ 58, 66.

[78] See §§ 87, 96 of the Defense Regulations (Emergency), 1945.

[79] See § 86 of the Defense Regulations (Emergency), 1945.

[80] For a discussion, see CF 538/89 Warshavski v. IP, Decision 44 (2), 870 (The printing press printed Popular Front training brochures. The appellant was convicted of an offense in pursuance of Regulation 85(1)(g) of the Defense Regulations (Emergency), 1945.

[81] The term publication for the purposes of the Ordinance is defined in the Penal Code Law, 5737–1977, in § 34 (24): "Publication – document, printed matter, computer material, or any other visual exhibit, and all audio means, liable to raise words or ideas, either alone or with the use of any means."

interpreted the Ordinance in a restricted sense, due to its direct infringement of basic rights, such as freedom of speech.[82]

Another restriction of free speech exists in the Press Ordinance, which requires a license from the Minister of the Interior for the publication of a newspaper and grants the Minister the power to close a newspaper.[83] It seems that in light of the infringement of freedom of speech, the law should not be interpreted on a broad basis. Accordingly, the Ordinance does not apply to the Internet and a license is not required for setting up an Internet site. There does not seem to be any disagreement on this position.

3.2.2 Enforcement of Hacking Prohibitions

Cyber-crime is perceived by many as less serious than ordinary crime. This distinction derives from the fact that hacking requires great sophistication and technological know-how and that such crimes are perpetrated by people sitting in front of a screen and typing, rather than by physically assaulting others. In addition, the damage caused by hackers is less concrete than the damage caused by such acts as breaking into a bank safe. In many places, hackers are considered cultural heroes, not criminals. Nonetheless, cyber-crime can have serious implications and requires special handling.

Accordingly, the Computers Law, 5755–1995, was promulgated[84] following the work of an inter-ministerial, interdisciplinary team appointed by the Minister of Justice. The law addresses several computer-related areas.[85] The need for legislation arose as a result of the increase in cyber-crime and the difficulty of adapting existing laws to incorporate the misuse of computers. Chapter 2 of the law deals with the handling of cyber-crime and the protection of abstract interests, which had no direct solution in legal provisions existing prior to this law. The use of the term "unlawful"

---

[82] See HCJ 547/98 Noam Federman v. the Israeli Government, Tak. Supr. 99 (4), 314; CF (Jerusalem) 557/96 IP v. Arieh Bar Yosef, Tak. Shal 98 (2), 762.

[83] The discussion in of the Kol Ha'Am Affair was based on this power. See HCJ 73/53 "Kol Ha'Am" Ltd. v. the Minister of the Interior, Decision 7, 871. Also in this matter, see HCJ 644/81 Omer International Inc. v. the Minister of the Interior, Decision 36 (1), 227 (appeal against an order for the cessation of publication of the Hameshiv newspaper). The order was issued by virtue of the Press Ordinance after the newspaper published praise of terror acts.

[84] Computers Law, 5755–1995.

[85] The Computers Draft Law, 5754–1994, DL 2287 (of 13.6.94).

in some of the sections of this chapter means transfer of the onus of proof to the prosecution.[86]

In rulings that discussed the Computers Law, two sections in particular have been referenced: Section 2 (disrupting or interfering with a computer or computer material) and Section 4 (unlawfully penetrating computer material). In the Refaeli case, it was decided that Refaeli transgressed §§ 2 and 4 of the Computers Law.[87] The court ruled that the deletion of useless computer material is a crime and that it is unnecessary to prove that the deletion caused damage or disruption to the computer.

In the Badir case, the accused committed offenses through the automated telephone system and were convicted of unlawful penetration of computer material.[88] The court ruled that there was no need to prove damages for conviction of this offense. It was also established that it is not necessary for the penetration to involve expertise in computer operation and software; it is possible for the offense to be committed by an innocent agent or a person fooled by the accused.

Ehud Tennenbaum, the "Analyzer," was sentenced to 6 months' community service and a fine of NIS 75,000 for hacking into the US Pentagon computers.[89] It was ruled that he transgressed §§ 2 and 4 of the Computers Law. The State appealed the leniency of the sentence. In the notification of appeal (CA 71227/01), the State sought to have a heavier sentence imposed on Tennenbaum for deterrence purposes. In the State's opinion, the lightness of the sentence conflicted with the values of just punishment, deterrence, and protection of public safety and security (particularly during an era in which there is a computer in every single field of modern life). The State also argued that, given the ease of committing cyber-crimes and the low probability of being caught, heavier penalties must be imposed to serve as a deterrent to potential lawbreakers.

Another difficulty in enforcement is that sometimes the offense is international insofar as the person committing the crime is using servers located overseas, while the country in which he lives has only an

---

[86] Boaz Guttman, "Hakikat Mahshevim Veyisumah" (Computer Legislation and Implementation), Mishpat Vetzava: Bitaon Hamaarekhet Hamishpatit BeZAHAL 13 (1999), 175–185.

[87] CF (Jerusalem) 3813/99 IP v. Oded Refaeli, Tak. Supr. 2000 (2), 1091.

[88] CF 40250/99 IP v. Badir (hereafter: Badir Case). It was also established in the ruling that modern telephone switchboards constitute a computer, as defined in the Law, and that infiltrating a voice mailbox and listening to the messages left there constitutes prohibited secret monitoring.

[89] Criminal Case (Kfar Saba) 3709/00, State of Israel v. Ehud Tennenbaum, Tak. Shal. 3709 (2), 41.

incidental connection with the overseas servers.[90] Section 140 of the
Emergency Defense Regulations stipulates that a person disturbing a
policeman or a member of the government forces in fulfilling his duty is
committing a crime.[91] Hackers penetrating government or army Internet
sites can be convicted of this crime.

3.3 Israeli Regulation of Encryption

The basis for the legal regulation of encryption in Israel was established in the subordinate legislation that followed the Control of Products
and Services Law, 5718–1957 (hereinafter: the empowering law).[92] By
authority of this law, in 1974 the Defense Minister issued the Control of
Commodities and Services (Engagement in Means of Encryption) Order,
5734–1974,[93] and the Control of Commodities and Services (Engagement
in Means of Encryption) Declaration, 5734–1974.[94] The arrangements
established in these regulations required a person to obtain a license before
having any involvement in the means of encryption. In 1998, a significant amendment was applied to the existing arrangement, making certain activities in encryption permitted occupations that did not require any
license. Additionally, the law now established three levels of license for
involvement in the means of encryption.[95] This change was an indication
that Israel had moved away from imposing a blanket prohibition on any
involvement in encryption methods without a prior license in favor of a

---

[90] Boaz Guttman, "Averot Mahshev – Etgar Hadash" (Cyber-crimes – A New Challenge).
http://www.psakdin.co.il/fileprint.asp?FileName=/Ip/Public/art_bduc.htm A distinction exists
between a computer offense (an action whose object is to prejudice the actual computer or
computer network) and an offense in pursuance of the Prevention of Terror Ordinance (where
the computer serves as a tool for committing the crime, for instance, a Hamas activist managing
activities of the members from an encrypted PC in the offices of an association masquerading
as a charity).

[91] Defense Regulations (Emergency), 1945.

[92] Control of Products and Services Law, 5718–1957, Sefer Hukkim 240, at 24. The subordinate legislation is by virtue of §§ 4, 5, 15, and 43 of the law, which appear as an appendix to
this report (herein: the empowering law).

[93] Control of Commodities and Services (Engagement in Means of Encryption) Order,
5734–1974, Kovetz Takanot 5735, at 45 (the Code Order).

[94] Control of Commodities and Services (Engagement in Means of Encryption) Declaration,
5734–1974, Kovetz Takanot 5735, at 46 (the Declaration)

[95] Sections 1(3) and 3 of the Control of Commodities and Services (Engagement in Means
of Encryption) (Amendment) Order, 5748–1998, Kovetz Takanot 5748, at 1107 (the amended
Code Order).

more liberal policy of limited control. However, it is important to note that there is a significant gap between the legal authority granted under the law regarding the licensing of encryption and the policy adopted in practice, which is much more moderate.[96]

3.3.1 The Framework of the Legal Arrangements up to 1998

The application of the empowering law, under which the subordinate legislation regulating encryption was promulgated, is dependent on the existence of a state of emergency in the country.[97] This law is a framework law, granting the ministers or any member of the government[98] broad authority to regulate, by Order, the production, sale, consumption, and use of a product or service,[99] provided only that there is reason to believe that such action is necessary to maintain an essential activity, prevent speculation, or prevent the public from being defrauded.[100]

As can be seen from its legislative history, the aim of the law is to assist the government in regulating the country's economy in times of emergency, ensuring the economy's development and growth and protecting the citizens from inequity. In emergency situations, this usually takes the form of black marketeering, speculation, hoarding, or price increases.[101] In light of this aim, the question arises as to whether the regulation of encryption, which is a security issue, should be carried out under this law.[102] Although "essential activity," which justifies the minister's intervention, includes action to protect the security of the State and

---

[96] See Mediniut Pikuah VeRishui Emtzai Hatzpanah Mishariim [Policy for Control and Licensing of Commercial Means of Encryption] (Director-General, Ministry of Defense, September 24, 2000) (Ministry of Defense Policy). Available at: http://www.itpolicy.gov.il/topics/docs/mediniyut_hatspana_mod.pdf.

[97] Section 2 of the empowering law. In the past, a state of emergency was declared under § 99(a) of the Law and Order Ordinance, 5708–1948, and currently under § 49 of the Basic Law: The Government. The state of emergency has never been cancelled.

[98] In accordance with the definition of "Minister" in § 1 of the empowering law.

[99] Section 5 of the empowering law.

[100] Section 3 of the empowering law.

[101] Divrei HaKnesset 21 (5717) 103–105.

[102] See, for example, Barukh Beracha, Mishpat Minhali [Administrative Law] (Volume 1 m 5747) 87–88. The author criticizes the broad powers given to ministers to issue regulations under the Control of Products and Services Law, in the absence of substantial parliamentary review. In the author's view, the state of emergency has sometimes served as a cover for the use of legislative authority under the Control of Products and Services Law, without any connection to the actual existence of a state of emergency.

the public,[103] the intention of the legislature was to provide the tools for dealing with the economic situation in a state of emergency.[104] Therefore, it may be argued that, in light of the principles of administrative law, we have here an overstepping of authority.

The broad authority granted to the ministers to issue Orders under the empowering law is subject to judicial review.[105] In the Knesset debate that took place when the law was adopted, it was proposed that a parliamentary review mechanism be set up in addition to the judicial review. According to that proposal, Orders that have legislative effect would be brought for the approval of the Knesset's Finance Committee, and the latter would be entitled, where it saw fit, to request the Knesset to repeal such orders.[106] This proposal was not accepted, leaving the judicial review mechanism as the only one that exists with respect to a minister's authority to issue Orders.[107]

Based on §§ 4, 5, 15 and 43 of the empowering law, in 1974 the Defense Minister enacted subordinate legislation dealing with the issue of encryption, as previously described. The empowering law establishes the principles of the policy and its parameters. The Control of Commodities and Services Order and Declaration are subordinate legislation that the executive branch may enact by virtue of specific authority granted under the law.[108] In general, the executive branch has the authority to establish secondary arrangements. In practice, the legislature may hand over the

---

[103] "Essential activity" is defined broadly, in § 1 of the empowering law, as "an activity which appears to the Minister to be essential for protection of the State, for public security, to maintain orderly supply of goods or services, to establish stability in the prices of commodities or the fees for services, to increase exports, to absorb immigrants, or for the rehabilitation of discharged soldiers or war disabled."

[104] As can be seen from the statement by the Knesset Finance Committee chairman, MK Binyamin Avniel, when he presented the law before the Knesset plenum for its second reading. Divrei HaKnesset 23 (5718) 421.

[105] Amnon Rubinstein & Barak Medinah, HaMishpat HaConstitutzionali shel Medinat Yisrael [The Constitutional Law of the State of Israel] (Volume 2, 5th ed., 5747), 812–833, 1165–1170. Judicial review examines the Minister's discretion in issuing the Orders in general, whether he used his authority for one of the purposes defined in § 3 of the empowering law, and whether the aim of the Order is related to the existence of a state of emergency. In the authors' view, the trend toward applying judicial review to the use of emergency powers under the empowering law will increase after enactment of the Basic Law: Freedom of Occupation.

[106] Divrei HaKnesset (5718) 421–422, statement of MK Binyamin Avniel.

[107] Divrei HaKnesset (5718) 429–430.

[108] Section 1 of the Interpretation Ordinance [New Version], which is the definitions section, includes under the term "Takanah" [Regulation] both Order and Declaration. An Order and a Declaration are different types of regulation, which the executive branch may issue as subordinate legislation. The difference between an Order and a Declaration is that an Order applies specific provisions for the implementation of general provisions found in the law, while a Dec-

authority to enact primary arrangements. Regulations of this nature are called *prater legem* ("outside the law") regulations, as they establish the provisions to carry out the arrangement established in the law, in addition to outlining the arrangements and principles beyond those established in the law.

In such cases, the primary legislator is content to set the goals. The achievement of these goals requires subordinate legislation. The bulk of economic legislation is of this type, which gives the secondary legislator a great deal more freedom of action by empowering the Minister to establish extensive economic controls through the issuing of Orders. The law details the means of control and the aims for which the authority may be used, but does not determine the arrangement for the content of such control.[109]

Our case is similar. The Code Order applies the provisions to be implemented regarding the licensing of engagement in the means of encryption. The Declaration gives notice of the products that are subject to control: data, means of encryption, encryption methods, encryption keys, records relating to encryption, and the engagement in means of encryption. It appears that the Code Order was aimed at providing a balance between the need to protect the national security of the State of Israel and the desire to allow reasonable competition within the Israeli encryption market without onerous restrictions on producers and users.[110] The key principle established in the Code Order is that a license must be obtained before one can engage in the means of encryption.[111] The authority to grant permits and licenses is vested in a "Director," appointed by the Minister of Defense. In practice, the Director-General of the Ministry of Defense is appointed to this position and then delegates his authority to the Supervisor of Military Export Controls.[112]

The Director has the authority to enter any establishment where engagement in means of encryption may take place, examine the means of encryption, and request additional details from the license applicant, both

---

laration has a declarative nature – it informs or announces, but does not contain provisions for implementation.

[109] See Rubinstein & Medinah, *supra* note 105, at 803.

[110] As stated in § 1 of the Ministry of Defense Policy.

[111] See § 2(a) of the Code Order. Engagement in means of encryption is defined in § 1 of the Declaration in the broadest terms, including development, production, possession, use, import, export, transport, transfer, distribution, sale, or acquisition of means of encryption, encryption methods, or encryption keys.

[112] Section 1 of the Code Order. Until the amendment in 1998, the Director was the IDF Chief Communications, Electronics and Computers Officer. See the Ministry of Defense website: http://www.mod.gov.il

prior to deciding on the license application and after the license has been granted.[113] Although the Director has extensive authority regarding the granting of the license,[114] the way in which this authority is used by the Director and the decisions themselves are subject to judicial review on the grounds of administrative law.[115] Of particular note among these are the grounds of reasonableness and proportionality, as well as subordination to the Basic Laws.

3.3.2 The Framework of the Legal Arrangements After 1998

Beginning in 1998, critics argued that that the Code Order and Declaration were too broad in light of the technological realities of the time. Two areas in particular were the definition of the means of encryption subject to controls (at the time, the Order applied to all means of encryption, even the simplest) and the range of activities subject to control (the definition was so general that it could have been argued that even the study of Biblical encryption methods was subject to control). A recommendation was made that the legislation applying to encryption in Israel be amended to adapt to the changing circumstances. Another recommended that a scale of licenses be established for engaging in encryption. A general license would be required for the use of encryption measures for identification purposes, while ensuring that these measures could not be modified to allow the encryption of data. Also needed was the establishment of a license to deal in data encryption measures, taking into account the balance between security considerations, commercial and Internet reliability issues, and the individual's freedom to protect his own privacy.

In light of technological developments and the increasing criticism of the sweeping limitations imposed by the Code Order and Declaration, a significant change was made in 1998 in the subordinate legislation applying to encryption[116] – the Control of Commodities and

---

[113] Section 6 of the Code Order.

[114] Section 5 of the Code Order: "The Director is entitled to issue the license, refuse to issue it, establish conditions for its issuance, suspend or revoke it, as he sees fit."

[115] For the extent of judicial review on the use of powers by an administrative authority, see Rubinstein & Medinah, *supra* note 105, at 347–359.

[116] For further details, see Victor Bognim, "Tashtit Mishpatit LeMishar Electroni [Legal Infrastructure for Electronic Commerce]", Sha'arei Mishpat 1 (5748), 169. See also Brian Nigan & Itzik Yarhi, "Skirah Mekutzeret – Kod HaTzofen [Brief Overview – The Encryption Code]" (1997).

Services (Engagement in Means of Encryption) (Amendment) Order, 5748–1998,[117] and the Control of Commodities and Services (Engagement in Means of Encryption) (Amendment) Declaration, 5748–1998.[118] Passage of these amendments followed the report of the Knesset's Subcommittee for Information and Computer Technology on Data Protection, in which the committee pointed out a number of problems in the existing legal arrangements that required legislative and governmental intervention. The committee noted that the Code Order remained in force mainly for security reasons and because of the desire to keep sophisticated encryption technology in the hands of the security authorities.

However, in light of the current availability of encryption technologies to anyone who wanted them, any attempt at sweeping control of the various dealings in encryption measures no longer seemed appropriate. The committee found that the Order, in its 1974 format, prohibited various uses of encryption measures, which, in fact, were freely available on the market. The Code Order created a situation in which citizens and organizations using those products were actually breaking the law, while others refrained from using existing measures and thus were prevented from competing in the global market. Regarding data protection, the report stated that the Order limits the ability to use data protection measures within the development of governmental information systems. As for the development of electronic commerce, the committee pointed out that a literal application of the Code Order's provisions did not allow the use of encryption technologies, their application or export.

Therefore, the committee recommended limiting restrictions on the export of the means of encryption, while leaving them in place only for countries defined as a security threat to Israel. The committee recommended a fundamental change in the legislation applying to the use of and dealings in encryption measures. This change was deemed essential in order to adapt the legal position in Israel to economic and commercial developments. First, it was recommended that the criteria pertaining to encryption products that were free of control or restrictions on their use and export be delineated. Second, it was recommended that amendments be made to the Code Order, which, in 1974, had applied sweeping definitions, restrictions on internal and external uses of encryption, and a bureaucratic procedure for obtaining a license. Third, the committee

---

[117] Control of Commodities and Services (Engagement in Means of Encryption) (Amendment) Order, 5748–1998, Kovetz Takanot 5748, 1107 (the amended Code Order).

[118] Control of Commodities and Services (Engagement in Means of Encryption) (Amendment) Declaration, 5748 1998, Kovetz Takanot 5748, 1109 (the amended Declaration).

recommended that a law be enacted to regulate the general authority and responsibilities for the control of encryption measures. They also recommended the establishment of the Data Protection Authority, which would make as much government information available to the public as possible, while maintaining the security of governmental data systems. In addition, it was recommended that a supra-departmental body be set up to deal with threats to national data systems networks.[119]

Not all of the committee's recommendations regarding amendment of the Order were implemented. Following are the key changes that were adopted in 1998:

1. Transfer of the sole authority for the control of the means of encryption and the granting of licenses to engage in the means of encryption to the Director-General of the Ministry of Defense.[120]
2. Empowerment of the Director to declare a means of encryption as a "free means." A "free means" is a means of encryption for which a general license has already been granted. A "free means" can also be a means that has been removed from the category of controlled items, and therefore dealing in it does not require a license.[121].
3. The granting of an exemption from a license for any dealing in a free means of encryption, with the exception of development, production, modification, and integration of a free means of encryption.[122] In addition, the granting of an exemption for any purchase, use or possession of a means of encryption, if the sale or transfer of the means of encryption to the person concerned was carried out with a license from the Director-General.
4. The creation of a scale of licenses for dealing in the means of encryption, as opposed to the original Code Order and Declaration, which did not contain such a list of classifications.[123] The amending Order does not define the criteria for licensing the use of encryption measures.

---

[119] The State Comptroller's report No. 52a indicates that within the General Security Service, there is a body called the National Data Protection Authority. The Ministry of Finance runs the Tehilah Project, which is one of the bodies involved in implementing data protection. Tehilah was established at the recommendation of the National Data Protection Authority and operates under its direction.

[120] Section 1(2) of the amended Code Order.

[121] Section 3 of the amending order, which adds § 3b to the Code Order. For example, the Director defined the Internet browsers Internet Explorer and Netscape Navigator, and the programs Microsoft Office and Winzip, as free means. http://www.mod.gov.il/modh1/encryption/tzofend.htm

[122] Section 3 of the amending order, which adds § 3a to the Code Order.

[123] Section 1 of the amended Order.

However, the scale of licenses that evolved includes a general license, a limited license, and a special license. The general license is granted for all types of dealings in encryption measures, with the exceptions of modification and integration. The more restrictive limited license is granted for certain types of encryption measures or for certain destination countries, based on criteria such as type of user. The special license is reserved for activities at the highest levels of encryption.

5. The definition of "class of user" of means of encryption includes a "financial institution, government institution, or incorporated body, institution, or organization of another kind authorized by the Director." It appears that this specific definition of the type of user results in a limitation in the control carried out under the Code Order. Unlike the general application of the Code Order to "any person engaging in the means of encryption," control under the amended Code Order would now apply to a specified or defined group of users.

6. The Order provides for the establishment of an advisory committee, one of whose members will be a public representative, and which will be headed by the Supervisor of Military Export Controls.[124]. The committee's task is to consider the applications for a license to engage in means of encryption. Where the committee recommends that the application be rejected, the Director will accept that recommendation and notify the applicant of the decision, providing the reasons for that decision. The Director is also permitted to delegate his powers to the advisory committee or to any subcommittee that the committee may appoint, with the exception of the power to grant, refuse to grant, rescind, or condition any license.[125] Moreover, the Order does not detail the licensing process.

7. Regarding the export of encryption products, the Order states that export permits will not be given for a limited number of countries. As part of the policy of controlling engagement in commercial means of encryption within the territory of the State of Israel, the Order provides that the holder of a license to sell encryption means must obtain authorization prior to selling such means to the Palestinian Authority.

The amended Order is an important stage in liberalizing control over encryption, and this trend is in line with the current trend in the Western world. At the same time, there is a gap between the policy adopted in practice and the legal framework, in that the policy actually adopted is even

---

[124] See the Ministry of Defense web site: http://www.defence.gov.il/modh1/encryption/index.html
[125] Section 4 of the Amending Order, which adds § 10a to the Code Order.

more liberal than the legal regulations. In our opinion, the present trend is desirable. However, the gap between practical policy and the broader legal authority has negative implications for the research and development considerations in the industry.

3.4 Freedom of Occupation

The legal regulation of encryption results in constraints for all those involved in the production of encryption programs. It is important to keep the fundamental right to freedom of occupation in mind when evaluating and creating laws that regulate encryption.[126]

The amended Control of Commodities and Services (Engagement in Means of Encryption) Declaration uses a broad definition of engagement, which includes, among other things, the "development, production, integration, acquisition, sale, use, and export of means of encryption." As stated in the Code Order, which implements this definition, "no person shall engage in the means of encryption except by license from the Director and in accordance with the conditions of that license." In practice, when beginning work on a new means of encryption, the applicant must submit an application for a license from the Supervisor of Military Export Controls in the Ministry of Defense. This license is necessary for all types of engagement in the development of encryption measures. Later, when the applicant has created the means of encryption, he/she needs to submit an additional application for a license for production, export, or sale.

In the case of the completion of development, a change in the product, or a significant version change, the applicant must submit, along with the application, a "working" version of the product, source code files, associated documentation and other materials that the Ministry may request. This is to allow the undertaking of a comprehensive examination of the product. At the end of this examination, the applicant will be granted a license or, as decided by the Director-General upon the recommendation of the advisory committee, will be sent a notice of rejection.

When a license expires, a company engaging in means of encryption is required to submit an application for license renewal. This application must be accompanied by a declaration that no changes have been made to

---

[126] Basic Law: Freedom of Occupation, 5744–1994, Sefer Hukkim, 5744, at 90. See also http://www.knesset.gov.il/laws/special/eng/basic4_eng.htm

the means of encryption. In cases of renewal of a license to sell the means of encryption, a report on the destination of sales must also be attached.

These procedures (e.g., elaborate requirements for obtaining a license) limit the freedom of occupation, which is explicitly established in the Basic Law requiring that all governmental authorities respect the freedom of occupation of every citizen or resident.[127] The requirement that anyone interested in engaging in the means of encryption must apply for approval from the Director-General of the Ministry of Defense casts a heavy shadow on the Ministry's commitment, as a governmental authority, to respect the right of an individual to freedom of occupation. As noted previously, the policy adopted in practice by the Supervisor of Military Export Controls infringes less on freedom of occupation.

The Control of Commodities and Services (Engagement in Means of Encryption) Order (Code Order) of 1974 was issued by the Minister of Defense under the Control of Commodities and Services Law, 5718–1957. In its original formulation, in 1974, a basic restriction on engaging in the means of encryption was imposed, as follows: "No person shall engage in the means of encryption except by license from the Director and in accordance with the conditions of that license." There is no doubt that this is a legal provision that was in force prior to the enactment of the Basic Law and remained valid until March 14, 2002 in accordance with the text approved by the legislature.[128] The Basic Law was enacted in 1992, quite some years after the Code Order was signed. As a result, there is a certain legal difficulty in treating the Code Order as void. However, according to the provisions of the provisional measures clause, the Code Order must be interpreted in the spirit of the provisions of the Basic Law: Freedom of Occupation.[129]

At the same time, the amended Control of Commodities and Services (Engagement in Means of Encryption) Declaration, does not benefit from

---

[127] *Id.*, Section 5.

[128] *Id.*, Section 10.

[129] In Supplementary Criminal Hearing 2316/95, Ganimat v. MY, Piskei Din 49 (4), 589, 654, Chief Justice Barak writes: "What is the anatomy of the influence of Basic Laws on the interpretation of old law? Obviously, the Basic Laws do not change the language of the old law . . .The only possible change can be in our understanding of it . . .The place for such change in the understanding of the old law is in the objective purpose of the item of legislation . . .In defining this objective purpose, we often have to balance between conflicting basic values . . .And it is here that the Basic Law carries out its interpretative activity. By virtue of it, a different weight may be given to the values and interests stated therein than was given previously. As a result, the balance between those interests and values that determine the objective purpose of the law may change . . ."

the preservation of laws section in the Basic Law.[130] This amendment contains a new definition of the terms "engagement in the means of encryption," which does not limit the violation of freedom of occupation rights. To a certain extent, it even widens it. The amended Code Order, also issued on the same day, makes use of the definitions contained in the Declaration and is not more lenient in its restrictions. In fact, the Code Order makes the procedure for obtaining a license more complicated and less certain, as it divides the types of licenses into three classes and appoints an advisory committee alongside the Director. The Director may delegate his/her authority in granting licenses to the advisory committee.

Perhaps these amendments of the Code Order ought to be subject to judicial review, considering that they are provisions that inhibit freedom of occupation. Judicial review has been carried out by the Supreme Court in a number of cases regarding legal provisions that contradicted the rights anchored in the framework of the constitutional revolution.[131] It has been determined that "the remedy for the unconstitutionality of the law is its annulment, and the authority for determining that unconstitutionality is given to the courts."[132] The right to judicial review in order to examine whether legislation is valid or void is based on the Violation of Freedom clause in § 4 of the Basic Law: Freedom of Occupation.

The limitation in our case is created by an "Order," which is quite low in the hierarchy of subordinate legislation. Perhaps the fact that the limitation is the result of an "Order" ignores the requirement that any limitation on a basic right be carried out by means of a law. It would appear that this distinction is not critical, given the rider in § 4, "or by such a law enacted with explicit authorization therein." The Order was issued by the Minister of Defense by virtue of the authority granted in the Control of Commodities and Services Law, 5718–1957.[133] Furthermore, it appears that the Code Order has a proper purpose and is in accordance with the values of the State of Israel. The security of the State and its citizens is a basic value that justifies regulating engagement in the means of encryption.

---

[130] Kovetz Takanot 5917.

[131] See for example BGZ 1715/97 Lishkat Menahalei HaHashkaot BeYisrael v. Minister of Finance, Piskei Din 54 (4) 367; BGZ 6055/95 Sagi Zemach v. Minister of Defense, Tak. Supr. 97 (4), 140; Civil Appeals 6821/93 Bank Hamizrachi v. Migdal, Piskei Din 49 (4) 221 (hereafter: Bank Hamizrachi Case); BGZ 1031/99, 1030, 1053, 1119, 1201 Cable et al. v. Speaker of the Knesset et al.

[132] See Bank Hamizrachi Case, supra note 131, at 418 (Justice Cheshin).

[133] Sefer Hukkim, 5718, at 24.

The main question in this regard is that of proportionality, and this in turn arises from one of the key characteristics of encryption products. Encryption products are dual use products in that they can serve constructive civilian ends, such as providing protection for personal information or commercial data; yet, they may also serve as a weapon in the hands of terrorists. In the Mizrachi Bank case, former Chief Justice Shamgar established three cumulative tests for determining the proportionality of a violation of individual rights: appropriateness for achieving the purpose, minimization of the violation, and reasonableness of the violation.[134]

3.5 Property Rights

Regulation of encryption has an impact on property rights, which enjoy explicit constitutional status in Israel.[135] The main effect is visible in the procedures that a license applicant is required to follow.[136] Here, too, the policy adopted in practice by the Supervisor of Military Export Controls is less offensive than what could be expected by the broad authority found in the subordinate legislation. However, in our view, not only should the practical policy be constitutionally valid, but it should be brought into line with the legal framework as well.

According to Israeli law, companies are required to submit the encryption program itself to the Ministry of Defense for examination. In practice, this means providing the source code files and disclosing the algorithms used by the encryption product in question. The Defense Ministry claims that, in practice, only a small proportion of companies are asked to divulge the source code.[137] However, since companies do not know ahead of time whether they will be asked to divulge their algorithms, this creates a "chilling effect." Also to be taken into consideration is the obvious damage done to the companies that are required to divulge their source code. In terms of proprietary concepts, this is a forced disclosure of trade secrets. Trade secrets, however, are protected under the law, both in legislation and

---

[134] See *Bank Hamizrachi Case, supra* note 131, at 347 (Chief Justice Shamgar).

[135] Basic Law: Human Dignity and Freedom, § 3.

[136] Control of Commodities and Services (Engagement in Means of Encryption) Order, 5735–1974 ("the Order"), § 2.

[137] Based on Yoram Cohen's comments at the Shefayim Conference.

in judicial rulings.[138] As in the case of other rights, the existing system of regulation and any future systems of regulation are subject to constitutional review. Given that property rights are not absolute, they may be violated under the terms of the limitations clause.

---

[138] See Commercial Wrongs Law, 5759–1999; BGZ 1683/93 Yavin Plast Ltd. v. National Labor Court, Piskei Din 48 (2) 244.

Chapter 4
Technological Issues

Mining information from the Internet requires mechanisms in two areas – decrypting secret communications that have been intentionally encrypted to keep their contents private and gathering data that is transmitted freely. In this chapter, we will describe the technical aspects of how these two goals are accomplished.

In our experience, it is crucial to promote and encourage an ongoing dialog between the technology innovators (engineers, mathematicians and computer scientists) and the guardians of the legal world (legislators, law enforcement officers and lawyers).

Although it may be less important for a parliamentarian or police investigator to understand the mathematical details of a particular encryption system, it is certainly part of his or her job to understand the limits to which the mathematician can guarantee various levels of privacy and security. As an analogy, he or she may also need to know some technical aspects of the "tumblers" of a physical lock and the strengths of various gauges of steel in order to have an effective dialog with the designers of safes and vaults. Simply stated, law making and its enforcement demand the convergence of security, technology and the law.

4.1 What is Encryption? The Technological Basis

Encryption has a long and interesting history. The word "encryption" comes from the Greek term, cryptography ("secret writing"). The use of encryption permits secret communications between two parties by means of a change – some sort of manipulation – of the information being

M. C. Golumbic, *Fighting Terror Online.*
© Springer 2008

transmitted. The two parties need to agree on the type of change and its details in order to ensure the successful transmission of messages.[1]

Within the world of defense, verbal messages of various types are transmitted – battle orders, intelligence data obtained from the enemy, as well as messages in text form. Traditionally, these texts were handed to encryption clerks, who were responsible for their encryption and transmission. The original text would be translated manually using some mathematical function – the key. The encrypted result would be transmitted by radio, by courier, and by advanced networks and satellites. The working assumption was that the enemy might be able to intercept the encrypted text, but as long as he did not have the key, the encrypted text was effectively immune to interpretation. Later, as encryption moved to mechanical devices and eventually to computer programs, encryption techniques entered a new era of sophistication and mathematical complexity.

Deciphering the intercepted message can be carried out at various levels by the enemy (also called the listener). Simply listening to the "live" transmissions is referred to as **passive listening**. Recording the messages and replaying them is called **active listening**. The most intrusive level of activity is when the enemy has the ability to insert messages of his own into the communications stream, or to modify messages before they reach their destination. The tactical advantage that this capability offers is obvious.

The most secret element of the encryption process is the key. Its length or complexity is of critical importance. It is helpful to compare the key used for encryption to a simple combination lock. In order to open the lock, one needs to select numbers in a certain order. If the key has a length of two digits, then there are 100 possibilities, three digits – 1000 possibilities, six digits – a million possibilities. To crack the lock, one must guess the combination, either at random, or by some systematic approach. This method is called "Brute-Force Attack."[2] The longer the key, and the more effort involved in cracking the code, the better the quality of the security. The effort increases exponentially with the length of the key, so a key

[1] This overview is based on the following sources: Andrew Tanenbaum, COMPUTER NETWORKS 577–621 (3rd ed., 1996); Scott Oaks, JAVA SECURITY 1–16, 289–328 (CA, 1998); Jonathan Knudsen, JAVA CRYPTOGRAPHY 1–27 (1998). Over the years, the use of encryption has played a decisive role in the battlefield. For discussion, see David Kahn, THE CODEBREAKERS: THE STORY OF SECRET WRITING (New York, Macmillan, 1967); (New American Library, 1973); (New York, Scribner, 1996). Comparisons among the three editions of that book illustrate the development of encryption theory and technology over time.

[2] See: Bruce Schneier, APPLIED CRYPTOGRAPHY: PROTOCOLS, ALGORITHMS, AND SOURCE CODE IN C, 151–54 (2nd ed., New York, Wiley, 1996).

of 64 to 256 bits is considered a sufficiently secure standard for most requirements. (In the commonly used ASCII code, a single letter of text is generally represented by 8 bits; in Unicode, by 16 bits.[3]) Encryption of texts permits letters and symbols to be treated uniformly, and so, when we refer to a "letter," we mean a letter or a symbol.

4.2 The Basic Principle of Encryption: Letter Replacement

One of the fundamentals of encryption is that of substitution, in which every letter is replaced by a different letter. This method was developed by Julius Caesar in his war against the city of Carthage. The key here is a string of 26 letters, related to the entire Latin alphabet. The number of possibilities for the key is 26! (26-factorial, a number approximately equal to a 1 followed by 26 zeroes). To break the key to such a code using the brute force attack method would require about 10^{13} years, assuming that the computer could calculate one result every microsecond.

In spite of this daunting time constraint, this encryption method is considered relatively simple to break, because of various statistical probabilities such as the high frequency of certain letters – e, t, a, o, i, n – and the frequency of certain letter pairs, such as th, in, er, re, an. Thus, one can assign the letter with the highest frequency in the encrypted text to the letter "e," the second most frequent letter to the letter "t," and so on, and then try to crack the key based on pairs and triplets.

4.3 Symmetrical Encryption

In spite of its shortcomings, the substitution method is the basis for the first important digital encryption method, DES (Digital Encryption Standard). DES was originally developed by IBM in the early 1970s under the name "Lucifer." The American government adopted DES in 1977.[4] DES transforms 64-bit blocks of source text into 64-bit blocks of encrypted

---

[3] In advanced computer environments, the Unicode system is used, in which each letter is represented by 16 bits (this allows 65536 possible characters). This method allows the encoding of characters from various languages, including those with non-Latin alphabets, using one universal protocol. See: Ken Arnold, James Gosling & David Holmes, THE JAVA PROGRAMMING LANGUAGE 8, 138, 277 (3rd ed., New York, Addison Wesley, 2000).

[4] For technical details of the Lucifer system, see J.L. Smith, *The Design of Lucifer, A Cryptographic Device for Data Communications*, IBM RESEARCH REPORT RC3326 (1971).

text, using a series of mathematical steps based on letter substitution with a 56-bit key.

When a particular block of text appears twice in the message, it will be translated into exactly the same block of encrypted text. For example, if the 64-bit word "Example 1" appears twice in the text, the encrypted translation will be identical in both cases. This consistency can be exploited to crack DES.

The original Lucifer system used a 128-bit key, but the United States National Security Agency (NSA) reduced the length of the key to 56 bits.[5] The NSA demanded that the exact algorithm be kept a secret. By doing so, the Agency would be able to decipher messages encrypted by this method, while other agencies (with the limited computing resources available at the time) would be incapable of breaking the code.[6] The issue of secrecy reached a critical point when the NSA cancelled cryptography conferences organized by the IEEE (the American Institute of Electrical and Electronic Engineers). The NSA issued legal orders, made threats and carried out monitoring to have the conferences cancelled because of the fear that certain secrets might be revealed.[7]

In 1977, two researchers at Stanford University, Whitfield Diffie and Martin Hellman, developed a model for a machine that could break DES and estimated that such a machine could be constructed at a cost of 20 million dollars.[8] Today, such a machine would cost no more than one million dollars. The machine compared a passage of regular text with a passage of encrypted text and would "run" 2^{56} possibilities until it had found the key.

In the early 1990s, two Swiss researchers, Xuejia Lai and James Massey, developed an encryption system similar to DES, but using a key length of 128 bits. They called the system, IDEA – International Data Encryption Algorithm.[9] Today, the patent for IDEA is held by Ascom

---

[5] The NSA has had reciprocal relationships within the world of encryption. In many cases, instead of a patent being registered for a certain invention or development, it has been requisitioned for the benefit of the Agency. For examples of such practices, see Kahn, *supra* note 1, at 672–736.

[6] The method was issued U.S. Patent #3,962,539 (8 June 1976).

[7] See: S. Landau, *Zero-Knowledge and the Department of Defense*, 35 NOTICES OF THE AMERICAN MATHEMATICAL SOCIETY 5–12 (1988).

[8] The exact description of the machine can be found in W. Diffie & M.E. Hellman, *Exhaustive Cryptanalysis of the National Bureau of Standards Data Encryption Standard*, 10 IEEE COMPUTER MAGAZINE 74–84 (June 1977).

[9] The method was first presented in: Xuejia Lai & James Massey, *A Proposal for a New Block Encryption Standard*, ADVANCES IN CRYPTOLOGY – EUROCRYPT '90 PROCEEDINGS 389–404 (1991).

Systems AG. At present, IDEA is considered unbreakable. Another similar method is called RC2/RC4. All of these methods work according to similar principles and are in general use throughout the world. These methods are referred to as "symmetrical encryption" or "conventional encryption" methods, because the two parties using the method utilize exactly the same key.

The weakness of symmetrical encryption. The weak link in all of the encryption methods discussed above is that the encryption becomes useless if the enemy steals the key. Given that the key for encryption and the key for decryption are the same, there exists a dilemma. On one hand, the key must be kept secret. On the other hand, it needs to be transmitted to all parties who need it, so it cannot be kept totally secret.

Despite this limitation, most encryption on the Internet still uses these methods, so both parties need to agree, prior to communicating, on the encryption method and on the symmetrical key they have chosen. It is clear that the first step, transmitting the key, cannot be secured by using the key because the key has yet to be determined.

4.4 Asymmetrical Encryption: Public Key and Private Key

4.4.1 The RSA Encryption Method

At just over 30 years old, the encryption procedure known as RSA is a relatively modern addition to the concepts of cryptography. Named after its three developers, Rivest, Shamir and Adleman, this method works on the principle of asymmetrical encryption – the sender and the recipient use different keys. In this method, every user has two keys, a **public key**, which is used by the "rest of the world" to send messages to the user, and a **private key**, utilized by the user to decipher the messages sent to him. The popular home encryption program PGP (Pretty Good Privacy) applies this method in an easy-to-use way.[10] Often RSA is used for the initial transmission of keys and then DES or IDEA, which are much faster methods, can be used.

---

[10] The program was developed by Phillip Zimmerman. A practical instruction book that describes how to get the most out of PGP is Simson L. Garfinkel, PGP: PRETTY GOOD PRIVACY 85–116 (New York: O'Reilly, 1995). The book also describes the history of the program and the problems faced by its developer.

4.4.2 Analysis of the RSA Method

It is worthwhile to explain and demonstrate the mathematical basis for the RSA method.[11] For this purpose, it is important to understand some fundamental concepts. A **computational problem** is a problem that accepts a certain input and calculates a certain output (the solution to the problem). There are two classes of such problems, depending on their complexity:

1. A problem is **tractable** if a method is known to solve it efficiently, that is, if there exists a fixed method, or algorithm, that can handle all possible inputs to the problem and solve it in a predictable (and relatively short) amount of time.
2. A problem is **intractable** if no known general solution exists that can solve the problem in a *controlled amount of time*. As we shall see, intractable problems can be utilized to create secure keys and to transmit data through public communications channels, as is the case with RSA.

Those sending messages to each other have additional information that will help solve the (specific) intractable problem immediately, while someone trying to crack the encrypted data (without the additional information) will encounter a problem that can be solved only by supercomputers running for hundreds of millions of years. In sum, for the intended parties of the communication, the problem is tractable, while for everyone else, the problem is intractable.

In the RSA system, which was first presented in a scientific journal in the United States in 1977,[12] there are three loci of information: the **sender** of the message, the **recipient** of the message, and the **public domain** (for example, the advertising section in a newspaper, or a non-encrypted area of the Internet). We will now demonstrate how the system operates in practice. This is the method that was protected by a patent that expired in September 2000.[13]

These are the *parameters* of information involved in the process:

---

[11] For further study, see: Thomas H. Cormen, Charles E. Leiserson & Ronald L. Rivest, INTRODUCTION TO ALGORITHMS 831–52 (Cambridge, MA, MIT Press, 1990).

[12] Ronald L. Rivest, Adi Shamir & Leonard M. Adleman, *A Method for Obtaining Digital Signatures and Public-Key Cryptosystems*, COMM. OF THE ACM 21(2), 120–26 (1978).

[13] U.S. Patent #4,405,829.

p, *q*: two prime numbers, selected by the **recipient** and kept secret.

They are not given to anyone else (not even the sender). The recipient can select them by means of a random prime number generator, because the test for determining whether a number is prime is a tractable problem,* as compared to finding the factors of a number, which is intractable.**

$n = p \times q$: The product *n* is placed by the sender in the **public domain**.

$t = (p-1) \times (q-1)$: calculated by the **recipient** and kept secret.

It is not given to anyone else (even the sender). This will be used afterwards to generate the private key.

E: a number whose highest common factor with *t* is 1 (in other words, it is relatively prime to *t*), calculated by the **recipient** (since *t* is known to him), and also placed in the **public domain**. Thus, *n* and *E* are a pair of public keys.

M: the message that the **sender** would like to send.

Again, it is easier to consider the message as a long string of binary bits (0, 1). If we treat it as a single binary number, its decimal value will be *M*. (The sender needs to check first that *M* is less than *n*.)

D: another piece of secret information calculated by the **recipient**, namely, the multiplicative inverse of *E*, using arithmetic modulo *t*, that is:

$$D \times E = 1 \pmod{t}.$$

Since *t* is known to the recipient, he can easily calculate *D*. The modulo operation gives the remainder after dividing by *t*. The recipient keeps *D* secret, and does not pass it on to anyone.

---

* There exist simple, speedy methods for generating large prime numbers. The question of whether a number is prime is a simple yes/no question. Gary Miller and Michael Rabin developed a series of tests that do this in a very short time (the Rabin-Miller method). See: M.O. Rabin, *Probabilistic Algorithm for Testing Primality*, J. OF NUMBER THEORY 12(1), 128–38 (1980). A prime number generator creates a large number, tests that it is prime using these methods, and if not, repeats the process until it finds a prime number.

** Finding the factors of *n* is much more complex than checking the primality of a number. This is the problem that needs to be answered in order to crack the RSA method. In order to answer it, one needs to check every number up to the square root of *n* to determine whether each of those numbers divides evenly into *n*. Although more advanced approaches have been developed, they have not improved performance times significantly from the method described. If *n* is a number of approximately 1000 digits, such a test, on the most powerful computer in the world, would take far longer than the age of the universe (by comparison, the universe's age, in seconds, is estimated at 2 to the power of 61).

In summary, we have the following:

The recipient has *D*, *t*, *p*, *q*.

The sender knows *M*.

Everybody knows *n* and *E*.

In addition,

D is the recipient's private key (to decipher the messages he receives).

E and n are his pair of public keys (to be used by all senders to encrypt messages sent to him).

To send the message: The **sender** takes the message M, checks the public keys n and E, calculates the encrypted message C and sends it through an open (unprotected) communications channel. The encrypted message C can be calculated mathematically as follows: $C = M \wedge E(\text{mod } n)$, where $\wedge$ stands for "raised to the power of."

It is easy to see that the sender does not have his own codes. In fact, he has nothing secret other than the message M itself. The encryption process is immediate.

To decipher the message: The recipient receives C, and can immediately extract the original message M, as long as he still has his private key D. The calculation is $M = C \wedge D(\text{mod } n)$.

Here is an example to illustrate the procedure:[14]

Preparing the keys:

The recipient selects two prime numbers p, q: say 2, 5, and calculates n: 10, which he publishes in the public domain. Of course, for practical purposes, the recipient needs to select values of p and q that are much larger (so that the enemy cannot easily factor n, the characteristic on which RSA is based).

The recipient calculates t: $t = (q-1) \times (p-1) = (5-1) \times (2-1) = 4 \times 1 = 4$.

The recipient then chooses (calculates) a number E that is relatively prime to t, in this example, relatively prime to 4. He may choose the number 3, since 3 and 4 are relatively prime (that is, their highest common factor is 1 – which meets the definition's criteria). $E = 2$, for example, would not work, because the highest common factor of 2 and 4 is 2, which does not fit the requirement that the highest common factor be 1.

The recipient places these two keys in the public domain: $E = 3, n = 10$.

Finally, the recipient calculates D: This is the multiplicative inverse of E, modulo t, that is $D \times E = 1(\text{mod } t)$. In our example,

$$D \times E = 1(\text{mod } t) \Rightarrow D \times 3 = 1(\text{mod } 4) \Rightarrow 9 = 1(\text{mod } 4) \Rightarrow D = 3$$

D is the recipient's private key, and he keeps its value (3) secret.

Sending a message:

Now, let us suppose that the original message, after conversion to bits is $M = 7$. This is the message that the sender wants to send to the recipient (of course, in practical applications, the numbers are much larger).

The sender calculates the encrypted message C by substitution in the formula $C = M \wedge E(\text{mod } n) = 7 \wedge 3(\text{mod } 10) = 343(\text{mod } 10) = 3$.

---

[14] See also: S.C. Coutinho, The Mathematics of Ciphers 33. (AK Peters, Ltd., 1999). This book describes the mathematical foundations of encryption theory and various algorithms for factoring numbers.

Note that the sender uses both public keys n and E to turn the original message M into the encrypted message $C = 3$.

Receiving a message:

When the recipient has received the encrypted message "3," he recreates the original message using the private key in his possession, $D = 3$:

$$M = C\,^\wedge D(\mathrm{mod}\ n) = 3\,^\wedge 3(\mathrm{mod}\ 10) = 27(\mathrm{mod}\ 10) = 7$$

The enemy has no way of knowing that the encrypted message $C = 3$ is in fact the encryption of $M = 7$, because he does not know the private key D (which derives from p, q, the factors of n). The decryption is complete.

The RSA method is based on the mathematical characteristic that the problem of breaking a large number into its factors is an intractable one. What does this mean? At a mathematical convention held in 1903, one of the speakers declared that the large number $2^{67} - 1$ was not prime, and, to convince his listeners, all he had to do was write: $2^{67} - 1 = 193707721 \times 761838257287$. It is obvious that the speaker had to work very hard to find those factors, but from the moment he found them, it was easy to prove his contention that their product is not prime. The problem is to factor large numbers such as $2^{67} - 1$, when one knows nothing about where their factors might lie.

At present, whole numbers of up to 200 digits can be factored within hours using a very powerful computer. However, if we consider a page of text, about the length of a printed page, then such a message contains about 8000 bits[15] which translates to a decimal number with 2400 digits,[16] significantly larger than the 200 digits that can be handled at present. Thus, an encrypted message of about a page in length is well into the the "field of intractable problems." Encrypted using RSA, as opposed to DES, such a page-length text would be virtually impossible to break.

The security provided by the RSA system is dependent to a large extent on the difficulty of factoring large whole numbers. If the enemy gets lucky and can factor the number n into its factors p, q, then he should be able to decipher the message. If we randomly select two prime numbers, each 150 digits in length, and multiply them together, we can create a public key n, 300 digits in length, that cannot be cracked within a reasonable time using the technologies available at present. Without a significant breakthrough

---

[15] A page of text contains approximately 1000 characters, which is 8000 bits (in the commonly used encoding system, ASCII, each letter is represented by 8 bits).

[16] 2 to the power of 8000 is 10 to the power of 2400.

in developing number theory algorithms, the RSA encryption system will still provide the highest level of security in the world of encryption.

While information is sent in coded and encrypted form online, there is also a great deal of material that is readily available on the Internet for those agencies who know how to gather it.

4.5 How is Information Gathered on the Internet?

4.5.1 General Background

There are three stages to intelligence work in the information age. In the first stage, an intelligence organization must identify the technological infrastructure that it wishes to penetrate. In some cases, this is extremely simple, such as the interception of an analog communication that can be received by a simple radio. In other cases, a complex and difficult task is involved. Such a task may require the development of a system for intercepting and decoding the desired broadcast by cracking sophisticated security mechanisms. Examples of this kind of task include encrypted on-line communications or hacking into computers protected by a firewall. In the next stage, the intelligence agency must actually intercept the transmission and listen in to it. This requires personnel who are able to handle transmissions in different languages. In light of the tremendous quantity of information sent online, sometimes computer algorithms can perform part of this monitoring task, identifying suspicious words in a text. Therefore, filtering is a critical element in intelligence work and a key tool in modern intelligence agencies' current war on terror. The third and final stage in intelligence work is the analysis, research and distribution of a finished intelligence product to intelligence consumers. This stage is less relevant to the current discussion. The three stages can be seen in the example of the work done by agencies such as the NSA, explained below.

Intelligence agency activity is, not surprisingly, secret. Accordingly, any information about this activity can be obtained only indirectly from articles published in the media. Journalistic sources[17] and various human rights organizations that monitor the activity of intelligence agencies[18] report that the largest intelligence agency in the world in the Signal Intel-

---

[17] See for instance: "Keshel Hamodiin Ha-Elektroni" (The Electronic Intelligence Failure) (Ynet): http://www.ynet.co.il/articles/1,7340,L-1116808,FF.html; Echelon: The Skies Have Ears (CNN): http://www.cnn.com/1999/TECH/computing/12/30/echelon.idg/
[18] See for instance the Echelon Watch of ACLU (the American Civil Liberties Union).

ligence area is the American NSA, the National Security Agency. This organization works alongside the CIA and the FBI and has equal status with them as a federal agency. It is also claimed that the US, in conjunction with other Western countries, operates a technological system that allows real-time interception of messages transmitted through many communications vehicles worldwide. This technological system is an international spy and wiretapping network called Echelon, which is operated by the NSA, in conjunction with the intelligence agencies of Canada, Great Britain, Australia and New Zealand. The original project was created in 1971, but its spheres of activity have gradually expanded since then.[19] According to the American Civil Liberties Union (ACLU) report, Echelon, which uses satellites, is installed today in one hundred and twenty wiretapping stations deployed in Seattle, West Virginia, Puerto Rico, Denmark, New Zealand, Canada, Australia, Holland and Cyprus.[20] The US has never officially admitted the existence of the system, but a European Union committee set up to investigate the subject of Echelon recently determined that the electronic spy network exists and even provided proof of its existence.[21]

The Echelon Project reportedly has a secret monitoring system installed in super-computers that can receive three billion electronic transmissions daily (according to estimates, approximately ten billion messages passed through the Internet daily in 2001). The report of the European Union committee investigating Echelon, was approved by the European parliament, strengthened suspicions that Echelon can receive and intercept communications of surfers around the world: telephone calls, faxes, satellite communications, e-mail, downloading of software from the Internet, microwave communications and fiber-optic transmission. In general, Echelon does not record calls but rather, "monitors" the system. For this, it uses "Sniffer" software programs. Sniffer is software

---

[19] The project was founded in pursuance of the UKUSA Signals Intelligence Treaty of 1948. Even though this is a secret treaty, references to it can be found in various Internet sources, among them highly credible sources. See, for instance, the reference to the treaty at the site of the Federation of American Scientists at: http://www.fas.org/irp/eprint/sp/sp_f2.htm.

[20] See the list of "suspected" listening stations, based on newspaper sources, experts in the field and books on the subject at the Federation of American Scientists site: http://www.fas.org/irp/news/1999/02/radome.htm

[21] Report on the existence of a global system for the interception of private and commercial communications (ECHELON interception system) – Temporary Committee on the ECHELON Interception System. See: http://www2.europarl.eu.int/omk/OM-Europarl?PROG=REPORT&L=EN&PUBREF=-//EP//TEXT+REPORT+A5-2001-0264+0+NOT+SGML+V0//EN&LEVEL=2

that "passes" over a main Internet server or telephone switchboard and examines all of its activity according to various parameters. Relevant communications activity is "retrieved" and transferred for continued intelligence handling. The Sniffer used by Echelon controls the information transmission on six main backbones on the Internet and collects information. This information is then transferred to a "dictionary," a collection of artificial intelligence software programs specializing in locating material of intelligence value. Echelon software locates messages containing suspicious words (e.g., "explosives," "Bin Laden," "Al-Qaida"), and seemingly innocent code words (known among the intelligence agencies as referring to intelligence targets), intercepts them, classifies them and sends them to the intelligence arms in the different countries.

4.5.2 Means of Collecting Information and Monitoring the Internet

For purposes of the legal discussion, the different Internet monitoring means can be classified according to the method by which the information is collected – either by monitoring or by hacking. Monitoring is the term given to recording operations carried out on the communications network by various users. Hacking refers to the computer server and recording the activities carried out on the server. The distinction between monitoring operations in the public sector and monitoring operations in the private sector (hacking into sectors that are the user's private property) has legal ramifications. Another aspect likely to have implications for the legal analysis is the type of information collected, be it the communications' contents, the communications log only, or general, statistical, demographic data on user groups in the system.

Information monitoring. Actual information monitoring consists of state-of-the-art wiretapping through a Sniffer, software that scans the service provider and examines its entire activity according to different parameters. The most recent, well-known and widely publicized Sniffer is the Carnivore.[22] Officially, the Carnivore was designed to help fight crime, pedophilia for instance. Naturally, however, it became a practical

---

[22] This name was given to the software by the FBI because it "chews" all the information, but "swallows" and "digests" only the specific information desired. Recently, in a public relations campaign, the FBI rechristened it DCS1000 because the actual name aroused criticism and violent public opposition. See the report at the ACLU site: http://www.aclu.org/news/2001/w021401b.html

tool for fighting terrorist organizations, which make frequent use of the Internet.

In general, the monitoring of Internet transmissions is carried out passively. Having identified the relevant packets it needs, the system monitors all the communications and extracts (while recording) the specific information in which it is interested. In the past, some have complained that the system is active, meaning that it itself implants information in the transmission, in order to render its activity more efficient. However, such a claim appears to be untrue. In practice, the monitoring is carried out on the Internet providers' systems. In many cases, the intelligence material collected by Carnivore is identical to the information recorded on the ISPs as an integral part of the operation of the Internet. Prior to September 11, 2001, a search warrant was required in order for this information to be transmitted to the investigating authorities. This situation changed following passage of the US Patriot Act.[23] When the FBI collects the information independently, the FBI plants the Sniffer on the ISP information nodes in a branch box. American ISPs have reported that even prior to September 11, the FBI tried to coerce them into installing Sniffer software on the systems that they operate. Several ISPs[24] and many human rights organizations[25]. campaigned against this infringement on privacy. The resistance to Carnivore lessened dramatically following the events of September 11. However, the ISPs still voiced some protest in the matter, particularly following the new legislation.[26]

Carnivore has two uses – content wiretap and identification of users – and it is likely that new and improved "carnivores" are now in development and use, functioning along the same fundamental lines.[27] **Content wiretap** consists of listening to electromagnetic or fiber-optic signals "broadcast" by the intelligence target and filtering the Internet communications from them, much like telephone wiretapping. Generally,

[23] See Chapter 2.

[24] See report on the ISPs' fight, for instance: MCI, EarthLink, AOL versus the FBI, in conjunction with the ACLU, in the Wall Street Journal of 14.7.2000. A report on the WSJ article can be found at ZDNET: http://www.zdnet.com/zdnn/stories/news/0,4586,2656409,00.html

[25] See for instance a letter from the ACLU on the subject of Carnivore to the members of Congress dated July 11, 2000, at the ACLU site: http://www.aclu.org/privacy/spying/15370prs20000712.html. Search the ACLU website for further references to Carnivore.

[26] See: "IT Workers Chew Over 'Carnivore' Bill" at the CNN site: http://www.cnn.com/2001/TECH/industry/10/11/carnivore.resistance.idg, and the continued public struggle conducted by the ACLU under the name: "Safe and Free in Times of Crisis" at the ACLU site: http://www.aclu.org/safeandfree/index.html

[27] The following technical information is based on Internet sources of varying levels of reliability, given the secrecy surrounding Carnivore. For instance: http://stopcarnivore.org and http://www.robertgraham.com/pubs/carnivore-faq.html

e-mail messages sent to and from the intelligence target will be intercepted. Activity in the e-mail account will be monitored, as well as all the incoming and outgoing traffic of a specific user, or a specific IP address. Federal court authorization is required to undertake this type of monitoring.[28]

Another use of Carnivore is for purposes of identifying the correspondents (**trap and trace / pen register**), including the location and identification of all those who contact or are contacted by the intelligence target. Location and identification include: identification of e-mail addresses, identification of the servers (Web, FTP) that the intelligence target uses, monitoring the users of an Internet page or a specific FTP site, as well as all the Internet pages or FTP directories to which the target has access. The use of software for the identification of correspondents without disclosing the contents of the correspondence is widespread, with few legal limitations on this use.[29]

With regard to e-mail, Carnivore monitors the exchange of information between two e-mail users, one of whom is the target. The Sniffer's primary interest is in the SMTP protocol created in this communication, which specifies the sender's address, the receiver of the message and the actual message made up of a **header** and a **body**. If the FBI has been authorized only to use **trap and trace** monitoring, then it is entitled to "listen" only to the first part of the protocol, containing details of the sender and receiver only.

The first part of the protocol is made up of data revealing the identity of the parties in the specific e-mail message. It might look like the following:

```
<-220 mx.altivore.com SMTP server.
>>>HELO mx.example.com
<-250 mx.altivore.com Hello [192.0.2.183], pleased to meet you
>>MAIL FROM: <alice@example.com>
<-250 <alice@example.com> ...Sender ok
>>>RCPT TO: <bob@altivore.com>
<-250 <bob@altivore.com>
>>>DATA
<-354 Start mail input; end with <CRLF>.<CRLF>
```

---

[28] See Chapter 2.
[29] See Chapter 2.

> > > (e-mail message)
> > > \ r\ n.\ r\ n
<–250 Queued mail for delivery
> > > QUIT
<–221 mx.altivore.com closing connection

The second part of the protocol is made up of a header and the body of the specific e-mail message:

From: "Alice Cooper"
To: "Bob D Graham"
Subject: Shipment
Date: Thu, 7 Sep 2000 15:51:24 -0700
Message-ID:
MIME-Version: 1.0
Content-Type: text/plain;
    charset="iso-8859-1"
Content-Transfer-Encoding: 7bit
X-Priority: 3 (Normal)
X-MSMail-Priority: Normal
X-Mailer: Microsoft Outlook IMO, Build 9.0.2416 (9.0.2910.0)
Importance: Normal
X-MimeOLE: Produced By Microsoft MimeOLE V5.00.2919.6600
How is the plutonium shipment coming? I need it by Friday.
–Alice

Compared to the Echelon project, Carnivore is a "surgical" Sniffer only. This means it cannot and does not monitor large-scale traffic from a large number of users. Instead, Carnivore focuses its monitoring on one person. This may be the reason for the surprising "openness" displayed by the FBI with regard to sharing information about the Sniffer, its capacities and its method of use. However, even if the intelligence agency's intention is to monitor the Internet traffic and e-mail of only one person, communications and computer agencies and artificial intelligence experts argue that the likelihood that the FBI will succeed "physically" in focusing on one person, or more precisely, on a single signal or byte, is almost zero. If this is so, then it is highly likely that the privacy of other users in the target's entourage may be invaded.

4.5.3 Collection of information on the server or the PC

There are several hacking means planted in the PC for information collection. The most widespread commercial means is the use of the technology called cookies. Cookies are a text file, stored by a website on the surfer's hard disk, which allows the recording and monitoring of the user's surfing habits, such as the sites that the surfer has visited, the advertisements displayed and whether he has responded to them. Originally, cookies were designed to prevent the inconvenience of repeat registration at sites that made use of them conditional on the sharing of personal details. Technically, planting the file does not require the user's knowledge, agreement or cooperation. Nonetheless, in the newer versions of browsers, it is possible to cancel the receipt of cookies, to change the browser definitions so that it will warn the user every time a site tries to send him a cookie, or to delete the cookies in the PC after each Internet connection.[30]

This technology does not in itself enable the collecting of information about the surfer, such as his identification by name or his physical address. However, the surfer himself frequently provides this information or defines it in the browser, and sometimes these details can be derived from the cross-referencing of several databanks. The commercial use of cookies raises serious questions concerning the protection of privacy, and this matter has been discussed frequently in the European Union.[31]

The Magic Lantern System. Another information gathering technique that has made the headlines and was subjected to public debate, after September 11, was Magic Lantern. This is a system used by the FBI for the handling of encrypted information on the computers of criminals and terrorists.[32] While information monitoring through Sniffers such as

---

[30] Programs that delete cookies provide a more efficacious solution against cookies. Software such as Guidescop and Burnt Cookies monitor the changes in the directory where the cookies are stored. Through them it is possible to delete cookies, to peruse the cookies on the hard disk and to decide whether to save them or delete them. The review is based on Gal Mor, "Ro'im Lanu et Hakol" (They can see everything) at: www.ynet.co.il/Ext/Comp/ArticleLayout/ CdaArticlePrintPreview/1,2506,l-234131,00.html. See also http://www.cookiecentral.com and Haim Ravia, "Al Glisha u-Pratiut – o al Ugiyot Bareshet" (On surfing and privacy – or on Cookies on the Internet) at: http://www.law.co.il/hebarticles/cookies1.htm

[31] See: Directive 95/46/EC of the European Parliament and of the Council of 24 October 1995 on the protection of individuals with regard to the processing of personal data and on the free movement of such data. http://www.cdt.org/privacy/eudirective/EU_Directive_.html

[32] The Magic Lantern was first revealed in the press on November 20, 2001 on the MSNBC communications network site: http://www.msnbc.com/news/660096.asp. The intelligence agency publicly admitted the use of Magic Lantern after media pressure only on

Carnivore has its advantages for the information-collecting agency, the difficulty of deciphering the collected encrypted material still remains. The Magic Lantern solves this difficulty for the intelligence agency, but at the same time arouses concern about the privacy of individuals and organizations.

The Magic Lantern is in fact keylogging software planted in the target's computer. The software can "see" the passwords keyed in by the suspect and thus, in fact, view the encryption key that he uses, allowing the simple and rapid deciphering of all encrypted material, from e-mail messages to credit card numbers. In order to plant the software, the FBI must go to great lengths to violate the privacy of the suspect. The software is in fact a virus that can be sent to the target by e-mail or by a third party considered reliable by the target. The virus can be inserted virtually in the target computer through other computer hacking means. Of course, there is also the possibility of physically planting the virus, by breaking into the suspect's home.[33]

When the software is present in the target's computer, the computer user is in fact in passive surveillance. The surveillance becomes active when the popular encryption application PGP (Pretty Good Privacy), in which the user must deliver a passphrase, is activated. In doing so, the target actually delivers the encryption key to the surveillance agent. It should be remembered that while the required content is protected by those keys, the actual keys are protected only by the password. The stolen keys allow the holder the possibility of decrypting, while the user is convinced that the keys are in his possession only.

Public debate has naturally focused on the question of privacy but has also questioned the legitimacy of a government activity containing elements that would be considered criminal if used by others, by hackers for instance.[34] The use of the software also raises the question of the handling of the "legitimate" virus by the various anti-virus companies. The FBI

December 12, 2001. See the report on the MSNBC network site: http://www.msnbc.com/news/671981.asp?0si=-. The FBI's first use of the software was in a Mafia case known as the Scarfo Affair. See the newspaper report on this affair at the abcnews.com site: http://abcnews.go.com/sections/scitech/CuttingEdge/cuttingedge011221.html. FBI assistant director Randall Murch admitted to the court that, when monitoring Nicodemo Scarfo, a mafia leader in New Jersey, FBI agents had broken into Scarfo's office and planted the software in his computer in order to steal the encryption keys. These keys allowed the FBI to decipher encrypted messages that served as criminal evidence against Scarfo.

[33] As was the case in the Scarfo Affair.

[34] See David Sobel, legal adviser of the Electronic Privacy Information Center) and Republican Senator Dick Armey at the MSNBC site: http://www.msnbc.com/news/660096.asp.

naturally attempts to persuade the companies to cooperate with it and not to "identify" the software as a virus, and there have even been rumors of cooperation agreements between certain companies and the American government.[35]

But where does that leave us? The technological capabilities of the FBI or the NSA may be far superior to the terrorist hackers, but many of the scientific principles under which they are operating, and the invasions they are capable of perpetrating, are similar. The legal challenges are in blocking the dangerous and unauthorized, while controlling those who are authorized with enforceable regulations. This is the conclusion that we discuss in the next chapter.

---

[35] Network Associates (www.nai.com), the manufacturer of PGP and the popular McAfee anti-virus software, was accused of having some sort of agreement of this kind. See the report on the affair and the company's denial at Wired.com: http://www.wired.com/news/conflict/0,2100,48648,00.html Robert Graham, the well-known computer security expert in Internet circles, writes on his private site www.robertgraham.com: "The official company position of any mainstream company is that they have no position. It would be bad business to help law enforcement invade customers' privacy, and it would be bad business to specifically work against the efforts of legitimate law enforcement. They are going to do their best to do neither." Available at: http://www.robertgraham.com/journal/020110-magic-lantern-position.html

Chapter 5
Recommendations: Is There a Need for New Regulations?

5.1 The Existing System's Suitability for the Internet

Is the existing system of checks and balances suited to the Internet? Are the checks and balances regarding security needs and the rights of the individual that developed in relation to wiretapping and monitoring in analog communications also suitable for the Internet? To our mind, the advent of new technology should not entail the abandonment of earlier values regarding the balance between privacy and security interests. New legal regulations (both legislation and case law), must be formulated with the characteristics of the new technology in mind. In particular, we wish to emphasize several unique characteristics of the Internet and its use that may be relevant when proposing new legal regulations:

1. "Digital tracks" – As already noted, the Internet is an information environment in which all communications and message exchanges constitute a type of data processing that creates a record. The monitoring possibilities are inherent and are activated routinely as part of the system's operation. For a telephone call to be monitored, a special wiretapping device must be installed. On the Internet, the contents of the conversation and the identification of the speaker and receiver are recorded automatically. In many cases, "monitoring" or recording will constitute a default. The safeguarding of privacy requires an active operation of deletion, cancellation, or prevention of the recording. Legally, this distinction is likely to have implications. For instance, the legal rule for telephone calls determines the circumstances in which wiretapping may be carried out (as is done in Israel under the Secret Monitoring Law). The application of checks and balances to the Internet requires formulating a definition of the circumstances that require

the prevention of recording information, the deletion of existing files, as well as restrictions on the uses, distribution, saving of data.

2. The digital environment is potentially very invasive, making the individual and his acts easily visible, and creating the possibility of unprecedented infringements of privacy. These invasive means enable the penetration of the private domain. A computer connected to a global network creates a kind of back door to the privacy of a person's documents stored on the computer. Recently, it was reported that by means of software planted in a PC through the Internet, it was possible to produce photographs of what happens physically in a person's home. Furthermore, monitoring software and databanks allow the collection of information about users in the public domain.

3. In the digital environment, there is a considerable difference between the expectation of privacy and the invasive reality to which the individual is exposed. This fact can be attributed to several factors:

- The average user is generally unaware of how potentially invasive Internet use can be. The invasive means are not visible to the user. The combination of software and hardware systems that may threaten privacy is only really known to those with above-average technological know-how and sophistication.
- The experience of surfing creates an illusion of privacy because it is done privately. In many cases, the surfer is in his home or his office, alone and not in public. Surfing is an independent activity, on the face of it, in cooperation with other people. Interactive services are experienced in the framework of a closed, intimate group. All these factors naturally increase the expectation of privacy.
- The frequent changes in the digital environment require routine updating of the means to counter the invasion of privacy.

Logically, through education and the dissemination of information, it is possible to lessen the expectation of privacy and to warn Internet users of their exposure to monitoring. On the other hand, the fact that the technology is still developing and changes at a dizzying pace is likely to reduce the effectiveness of these solutions.

5.2 Implementing Existing Legal Regulations for the Internet

What is the significance of implementing existing legal regulations to the Internet? The existing legal regulations in Israel, for example, distinguish between secret monitoring and search warrants. Secret monitoring that is regulated in the Secret Monitoring Law protects the privacy of the dialogue and requires an order of the President or Vice-President of a district court, which will be issued according to the conditions defined in the law. A search warrant, on the other hand, is in the jurisdiction of the Magistrate's Court. Search and secret monitoring differ as far as the awareness of the subject of the monitoring, the duration of the infringement and the effect on third parties. In the case of a search, this is a one-time infringement. The person is aware of the investigation and the infringement is focused on him and his belongings. Secret monitoring, on the other hand, is a prolonged infringement, without the knowledge of the person being investigated, which may violate the privacy of the suspect (through the "listening in" on personal communications not relevant to the investigation) and of third parties (such as other users of the telephone lines, and parties conversing with the subject of the investigation).[1]

In this context, what legal regulations should be applied to the Internet? Monitoring on the Internet appears more to resemble secret monitoring. This is an action carried out without the knowledge of the subject of the investigation, at times with only the cooperation of the service provider. This is also a prolonged activity, which may also infringe upon the privacy of other surfers.

5.3 Protecting the Right to Privacy

Our recommendations are based on the premise that the privacy of surfers must be safeguarded. The extreme technological changes inherent in the digital environment should not lessen the right to privacy or the protection of privacy. However, individual legal rules must be formulated, taking into account the special technological characteristics discussed above. Additionally, values of privacy must be built into the technology.[2] The absence of national frontiers on the Internet must also be taken into account.[3] It is clear that the public must be informed and educated about its right to privacy, the threats to this right and the way to handle these threats.

Another difficulty is that alongside the public threat to privacy (from the State), there is another substantial threat to privacy in the digital

---

[1] Lecture of Adv. Nava Ben-Or, Shefayim Conference (Dec. 27, 2001).

[2] See for instance the P3P technological standards and also: Lawrence Lessig, CODE AND OTHER LAW OF CYBERSPACE (New York, Basic Books, 1999).

[3] See David R. Johnson & David G. Post, Law and Borders: The Rise of Law in Cyberspace, 48 STAN. L. REV 1367 (1996).

environment, from commercial and private agencies. In this context, the question arises as to the extent to which the State must be restricted in its use of the same means that are accessible to private agencies. A separate discussion is required on the relationship between private regulation and public regulation. In this book, we merely wish to point out the difficulties.

It is clear that an individual's right to privacy needs to be balanced with the security interests of the public as a whole. We recommend action be taken to address the direct and indirect threats to individual privacy.

We therefore feel that the following approach should be adopted:

Regarding direct harm, measures should be taken that will permit the security authorities to respond to security needs, without exceeding the extent necessary.

- The purpose for which the infringement of privacy is permitted needs to be clearly and explicitly defined, and must be limited solely to the needs of thwarting terrorism. It should not be permitted for obtaining evidence after an incident takes place, unless there is the possibility of a repetition of the terrorist act, in which case the issue again becomes one of prevention.
- An independent, external, review mechanism needs to be established. It would be appropriate for this mechanism to be prior judicial review, similar to the position regarding wiretapping. We propose that any authority that requests the use of "back door" penetration or any other means of breaking encryption should apply to the court prior to doing so. The court may then consider the need for such penetration or decryption in light of the direct harm expected as a result.

Regarding indirect damage, the extent of the State's intervention in the production and importation of technological measures needs to be defined, as well as the extent to which the State is entitled to obtain access to "back doors." An explicit and narrow general arrangement regarding encryption may be effective in limiting the indirect damage done to individuals' privacy.

It should also be noted that the failure to provide law enforcement agencies with sufficient means of decryption ("back door" access) or the establishment of overly rigid criteria and procedures for obtaining permission for specific decryption operations could bring about an undesirable result that would do more harm to right to privacy of suspects and others. For example, instead of deciphering e-mail correspondence, law enforcement authorities might use cameras or personal surveillance, whose impact on a suspect's privacy is more extensive and less focused. Professor Michael Froomkin raises an alternative viewpoint that relates to encryption itself, even before any governmental intervention. Froomkin claims that the very use of key escrow violates privacy in two ways. First, there is now a third party involved in any communication: the party that issues the private and public keys. Second, when a public key needs to be recreated, certain personal information has to be provided (here the reference is to governmental agencies wanting to recreate a public key, not the owner of the key). This viewpoint is not related to the two threats to privacy which we have discussed (which are more closely related to governmental activities), but rather to the possible violation of privacy rights by encryption mechanisms or by the producers of encryption products.[4]

5.4 The Liability of Internet Service Providers

The first issue that must be placed on the legislator's agenda is an assessment of the need for legislation regarding service providers' liability for the harmful content of third parties. The assessment involves an examination of the actual conduct of the service providers in the absence of regulation. Does uncertainty cause undesirable results? It is necessary, for instance, to examine how a site storage service provider reacts to a complaint from a surfer about another site, or about the words of another surfer in a forum operated by that provider.

If the existing legal uncertainty leads to the practice of "private censorship," then the legal situation must be clarified through legislation. Such legislation must minimize the undesirable impacts discussed above. In particular, the discretion exercised by the provider must be defined as precisely as possible, leaving the provider with a clear and limited area of decision. In this way, one can minimize the "cooling effect" and the "itchy finger" of the provider to close sites.

Earlier we discussed several existing models delineating the liability of Internet service providers – full liability, full immunity, or conditional and restricted immunity. In our opinion, each of these models has a number of disadvantages. We feel that an approach of uniform regulation for different types of harmful content must be adopted, whether that content

---

[4] Michael Froomkin, *It Came From Planet Clipper: The Battle Over Cryptographic Key 'Escrow'*, 1996 U. CHI. L. FORUM 15, available at http://www.law.miami.edu/~froomkin/articles/planet_clipper.htm.

is related to defamation, infringement of privacy, infringement of intellectual property rights or terrorist propaganda.[5]

The general principle established in American legislation of immunity for intermediate agencies should be adopted, but it should be qualified with an exception. In order to protect individual rights and interests, an effective enforcement channel through action in court must be allowed for injured parties. In this sense, our proposal differs from American law. The court will be required to weigh the public interest or the rights of the protected individual, against considerations of public policies and interests. In this way, the moral checks and balances developed in case law will be safeguarded, and will not be privatized through the commercial service provider. The court's power will be limited to the issuing of injunctions only. Finally, as long as a court has not ordered a service provider to act, the provider will enjoy immunity from damage claims.

5.5 Regulating Encryption Products to Protect Freedom of Occupation and Property Rights

We now turn our attention to the considerations that should serve as guidelines in the formulation of policy regarding encryption and decryption, particularly with regard to the State of Israel. Apart from the security considerations that underlie the entire issue, there are economic considerations and human rights considerations. The economic considerations consist of, in the narrow sense, the market for encryption products or electronic commerce, and in the broader sense, intervention in the free market. Human rights considerations range from the right to privacy and the freedom of speech to property rights and freedom of occupation. An in-depth examination of these considerations will lead to a broader viewpoint and will assist in formulating policy guidelines for the most desirable legal arrangement.

We concur with the recommendations of the Knesset's Subcommittee on Israel's Preparedness for the Information Age to enact a law that regulates the authority and overall responsibility for controlling the means

---

[5] In this context the reason for the differential American approach is unclear. It derives apparently from economic and political pressures exercised by commercial lobbies. For a general discussion of the influence of lobbies on American legislation in the context of copyrights, see: Jessica Litman, DIGITAL COPYRIGHT (Prometheus Books, 2001).

of encryption.[6] Regulation of this issue in primary legislation is also appropriate, therefore, for reasons of separation of powers, and to provide effective review of the actions of the executive branch.

In our opinion, it is inappropriate to place the policy determination questions in the hands of the secondary legislator. The existing system of regulations regarding encryption is primary in nature. Therefore, it is appropriate that any changes to the regulations regarding encryption be established by the legislature. This is an additional reason for regulating the issue through primary legislation.

We believe that the trend toward liberalization should continue. The legal framework in Israel should be shaped taking into consideration this liberal reality and mindful of the following points:

1. The regulation of encryption by means of subordinate legislation, in the framework of economic law, is not appropriate. By its nature, this is a primary arrangement that has implications for basic rights. In practice, the policy that has been adopted establishes prohibitions and permits without specific legislative authority. The result is that the determination of policy is carried out by the executive branch without the direction of the legislator. From the point of view of the principles of administrative and constitutional law, this arrangement is highly problematic with negative implications, such as the "chilling effect" experienced by the industry. Therefore, we believe that the legal response to encryption needs to be established in primary legislation.
2. The aim of the legislation is to answer real security needs. These needs include safeguarding security and sensitive information, and protecting the surveillance and intelligence gathering measures used by the defense and security establishment. These needs are legitimate considering the accessibility and availability of encryption products. Therefore, this legislation has a worthwhile purpose, and is in line with the values of the State of Israel, as required under the Basic Laws.
3. The existing system of regulation and the proposed legislation have a negative effect on freedom of occupation and property rights. The existing system may harm the right to privacy, in addition to violating freedom of speech and the free flow of ideas in academic research. Therefore, the present system of regulation should be reinterpreted in

---

[6] The Subcommittee on Israel's Preparedness for the Information Age was established in 1997, in the framework of the Knesset Committee on Information and Computer Systems. It should be emphasized that the committee's report was published prior to the changes in the Code Order in 1998 (the Subcommittee for Information and Computer Technology).

the spirit of the Basic Law. The proposed legislation needs to meet the proportionality test in the Basic Laws of Freedom of Occupation and Human Dignity and Freedom.

In order to meet the requirements of proportionality, any system of regulation needs to be based on the characteristics of the products in question and the functions they are supposed to fulfill. It would be appropriate to distinguish, as much as possible, between different uses for encryption products. In fact, there exists a range of uses. At one end of the spectrum are products that are used solely for commercial use and have no defense applications at all. At the other end are products that are purely defense-oriented, with no civilian uses. Clearly, the bulk of products would be spread along this range, with the courts determining exactly where they lie.

Products leaning toward the civilian end of the spectrum should be totally exempt from regulation, such as products for the verification of digital signatures.[7] On the other hand, there is a clear need for the regulation of products at the other end of the spectrum, those with a defense or security orientation. As for the variety of products in the middle of the range, proportionality can be achieved by providing clearer definitions of what is permitted, by delineating what exactly is at the discretion of the authorities, and by carrying out judicial review.

In addition, the system of regulation has to distinguish explicitly between the aims of the producer of encryption products. Products that, by their nature, are for private use only should not be subject to any form of regulation. Consequently, the marketing of such products on the local market should be exempt from regulation. In order to achieve the security goals, restrictions may be applied to the export of the products that lie closer to the defense end of the spectrum.

Overall, our recommendation is to close the gap between the practical policy and the legal authority. Therefore, it would be worthwhile to examine the constitutionality of the existing regulations and not to rely on the fact that the present practice is less stringent. In order to meet the proportionality test, the law must clearly and explicitly define the extent of the regulation and the boundaries of the government's discretion.

A number of models exist for regulation. We believe that it is inappropriate to adopt a model in Israel based on a sweeping prohibition

---

[7] This already exists to a certain extent, with some means of encryption being defined as "free means." However, the number of encryption products currently classified as free is limited, demonstrating the lack of proportionality.

accompanied by specific exclusions. Recommended amendments to the current licensing model are as follows:

1. The extent of the government's discretion needs to be defined and limited to actual security needs. For example, the need to prevent terrorist activity should be a priority, as opposed to the need to obtain evidence for a crime after it has occurred.
2. The areas of activity that require prior licensing need to be defined. In order to achieve this, it is necessary to distinguish between private/civilian uses and defense/security uses. The uses falling in the first category should be exempt from any form of regulation. However, regulation is necessary for the products that are not clearly for private/civilian use. When regulation is needed, it should be subject to the following criteria:

    a. The aims of the producer should be identified.
    b. Licensing requirements are necessary to control the destination of the product. A distinction should be made between local marketing and export. Export controls are needed to prevent the product from ending up in the hands of foreign terrorists. Control of local marketing, on the other hand, is less justified, particularly when the product's purpose is closer to the civilian end of the spectrum.

The approval process for licensing needs to be defined. Limits are necessary in regard to the amount and type of information that the government is allowed to request from a producer seeking a license. The stages in the process for examining license applications must be fixed in law. The details of the examination process may be fixed in the subordinate regulations. An appeals process needs to be established for applicants whose request for a license has been rejected. Perhaps the appropriate context for such an administrative appeal is in the judicial review function of the Administrative Affairs Court. If this is the case, procedures need to be established to ensure the secrecy of the proceedings.

As for decryption, in the event that the relevant authority requests access to an existing encryption product via a "back door," a mechanism for prior judicial review needs to be created, similar to that adopted under the Secret Monitoring Law, 5739-1979.

Alternative models for regulation should be considered. One possible model is to permit the registration of encryption products without imposing prior control. This model is similar to the process for registering databases under the Privacy Protection Law, 5741-1981. Implementing such a model would impose one single obligation on the producers of an encryption product: the registration of its existence and the provision of general information about the product. The adoption of this model allows the government to be aware of the encryption products on the market and their producers. When the need to investigate a product arises, the government can apply to the courts for permission to do so.

Concluding Remarks

My friend and colleague, Larry Manevitz, interrupted me with a phone call while working in my office in the Eshkol tower building of the University of Haifa on September 11, 2001. "Something catastrophic is happening in New York." I immediately clicked on to cnn.com and news.sky.com and watched in horror as the situation developed. Thousands of miles away, weeping, my sister-in-law Judy watched the same scene, in person, live from her car at a safe distance, as the second tower imploded.

I had been booked on a flight that night from Israel to New York, and was scheduled to give a seminar talk at Rutgers University on September 13th. It didn't happen. Nothing since then has been quite the same.

The September 11th terrorists freely used the same Internet for their deadly planning that I (and many of you) used to watch the vivid, horrible shots of their actions. They continue to exploit the open underbelly of free society at every opportunity.

In a forthcoming book, "Terrorism Informatics: Knowledge Management and Data Mining for Homeland Security", edited by H. Chen, et al., the contributors describe some of the cutting-edge concepts, technologies, and practices that are being developed to meet today's worldwide challenges.[1] Collectively, the articles further emphasize the view that a wide variety of methods must be used in terrorism informatics, drawn from computer science, informatics, statistics, mathematics, linguistics, and social sciences, to cope with the huge amounts of information from multiple sources of varying types and in numerous languages. And as this book goes to press, a further advanced research workshop sponsored by

---

[1] Chen, H., Reid, E., Sinai, J., Silke, A., Ganoz, B., eds., TERRORISM INFORMATICS: KNOWLEDGE MANAGEMENT AND DATA MINING FOR HOMELAND SECURITY (Springer, 2007).

M. C. Golumbic, *Fighting Terror Online.*
© Springer 2008

NATO has just taken place on the same topic "Security Informatics and Terrorism – Patrolling the Web".[2]

The provisions of the law have changed rapidly since September 11. Statutes and regulations have been revised, strengthened, reinterpreted, or redefined throughout the democratic world. While the particulars of the law will necessarily vary, the fundamental issues, dilemmas and questions raised here will last far into the coming decades. The evolution of technology, breakthroughs in scientific research, and the relentless determination to fight the evil of terror must lead us, our children, and their children to find the solutions necessary to protect the individual and society from harm, and at the same time balance security and civil liberties.

It is a challenge that we must meet, and a fight that we must win.

---

[2] NATO Advanced Research Workshop, "Security Informatics and Terrorism – Patrolling the Web", http://cmsprod.bgu.ac.il/Eng/conferences/Nato/

Martin Charles Golumbic is Professor of Computer Science and Director of the Caesarea Edmond Benjamin de Rothschild Foundation Institute for Interdisciplinary Applications of Computer Science at the University of Haifa. He is the editor of the book "*Advances in Artificial Intelligence, Natural Language and Knowledge-based Systems*" (Springer, 1990), the author of the book "*Algorithmic Graph Theory and Perfect Graphs*" (second edition, Elsevier 2004), coauthor of a second book "*Tolerance Graphs*" (Cambridge University Press, 2004), and the founding editor-in-chief of the journal series "*Annals of Mathematics and Artificial Intelligence*" (Springer). Professor Golumbic received his Ph.D. in mathematics from Columbia University in 1975, and has previously held positions at New York University, Bell Laboratories, IBM Israel and Bar-Ilan University as well as visiting positions at Université de Paris, the Weizmann Institute of Science, and Ecole Polytechnique Fédérale de Lausanne. He has given guest lectures in 15 states in the U.S.A. and in 20 other countries, and he was elected as a Fellow of the European Artificial Intelligence society ECCAI in 2005.

Name Index

Subject Index

Printed in the United States
111443LV00003B/166-168/A

9 780387 735771